Beast ACADEMY

By Art of Problem Solving

MATH
PRACTICE
3A

Jason Batterson
Shannon Rogers

Published by: AoPS Incorporated
                   10865 Rancho Bernardo Rd Ste 100
                   San Diego, CA 92127-2102
                   info@BeastAcademy.com

ISBN: 978-1-934124-41-3

Written by Jason Batterson and Shannon Rogers
Book Design by Lisa T. Phan
Illustrations by Erich Owen
Grayscales by Greta Selman

Visit the Beast Academy website at www.BeastAcademy.com.
Visit the Art of Problem Solving website at www.artofproblemsolving.com.
Printed in the United States of America.
2018 Printing.

Contents:

This is Practice Book 3A in a four-book series for 3rd grade.

3A
• Shapes
• Skip-Counting
• Perimeter and Area

3B
• Multiplication
• Perfect Squares
• The Distributive Property

3C
• Variables
• Division
• Measurement

3D
• Fractions
• Estimation
• Area

For more resources and information, visit BeastAcademy.com.

This is Beast Academy Practice Book 3A.

Each chapter of this Practice book corresponds to a chapter from Beast Academy Guide 3A.

MATH
PRACTICE
3A

MATH
GUIDE
3A

The first page of each chapter includes a recommended sequence for the Guide and Practice book.

You may also read the entire chapter in the Guide before beginning the Practice chapter.

CHAPTER 1
Shapes

Use this Practice book with Guide 3A.

Recommended Sequence:

Book	Pages:
Guide:	12–17
Practice:	7–9
Guide:	18–25
Practice:	10–14
Guide:	26–33
Practice:	15–24
Guide:	34–41
Practice:	25–37

You may also read the entire chapter in the Guide before beginning the Practice chapter.

Some problems in this book are very challenging. These problems are marked with a ★. The hardest problems have two stars!

Every problem marked with a ★ has a *hint!*

Hints for the starred problems begin on page 94.

Other problems are marked with a ✏. For these problems, you should write an explanation for your answer.

54.
★

55.

42 Guide Pages: 39-43

Some pages direct you to related pages from the Guide.

None of the problems in this book require the use of a calculator.

Solutions are in the back, starting on page 98.

A complete explanation is given for every problem!

CHAPTER 1
Shapes

Use this Practice book with Guide 3A.

Recommended Sequence:

You may also read the entire chapter in the Guide before beginning the Practice chapter.

EXAMPLE | What type of angle is formed by connecting A to B to C?

A•   • C

•
B

Connecting A to B and B to C gives us the following angle:

A•   •C

B

The angle is **obtuse.**

When two lines meet, they make an **angle.**

If the lines meet at a perfect "L", the angle is a **right** angle.

An angle that is smaller than a right angle is called **acute**, and an angle that is larger than a right angle is called **obtuse.**

The corner of a piece of paper is a right angle.
You can use the corner of a sheet of paper to help
you figure out if an angle is acute, right, or obtuse.

PRACTICE | Use the diagram below to answer the questions that follow.

7/17

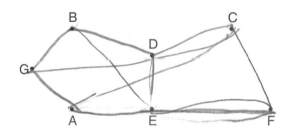

1. What type of angle is formed by connecting A to B to C?

1. _Light_

2. What type of angle is formed by connecting D to E to B?

2. _acute_

3. What type of angle is formed by connecting A to E to C?

3. _Obtuse_

4. What type of angle is formed by connecting C to F to E?

4. _acute_

5. What type of angle is formed by connecting B to D to C?

5. _obtuse_

6. What type of angle is formed by connecting B to G to A?

6. _right_

EXAMPLE

For the following mazes, trace a path from start to finish that has only *acute* angles.

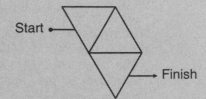

Start • Finish

In the solution below, all of the angles made by the path are acute.

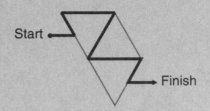

Start Finish

Each of the paths created below has at least one angle that is not acute, so each is incorrect.

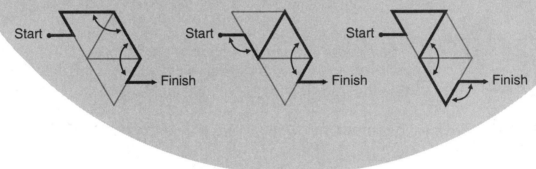

Start • Finish   Start • Finish   Start • Finish

PRACTICE | Complete each angle maze below by tracing a path from start to finish that has only acute angles.

Print more copies of these angle mazes at BeastAcademy.com.

7. Start • Finish

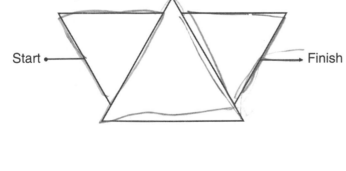

8. Start • Finish

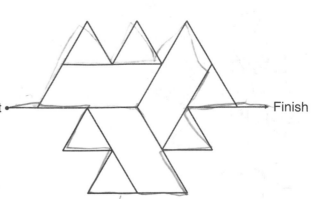

9. Start 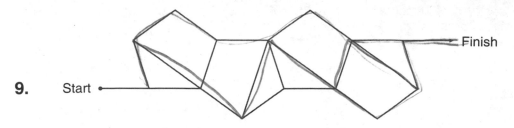 Finish

Be careful to avoid right angles in the next two mazes.

10. Start 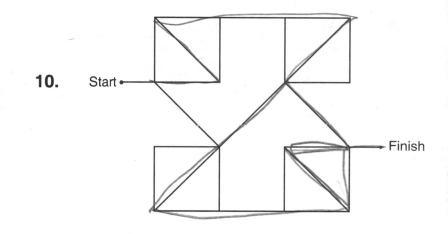 Finish

11. ★ Start 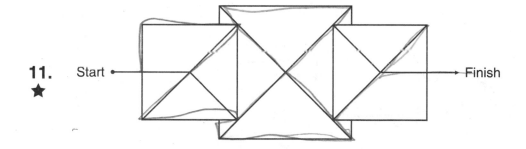 Finish

For problem 12, trace a path from start to finish that has only **obtuse** angles.

12. Start 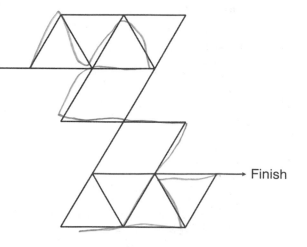 Finish

Triangles have three sides and three angles.

A triangle can be named by letters at its three corners. A triangle with three acute angles is an **acute** triangle.

A triangle with one right angle is a **right** triangle.

A triangle with one obtuse angle is an **obtuse** triangle.

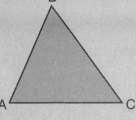

Triangle ABC is an **acute** triangle.

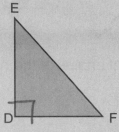

Triangle DEF is a **right** triangle.

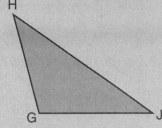

Triangle GHJ is an **obtuse** triangle.

When naming a triangle by the letters at its corners, the order is not important. Triangle ABC can also be named triangle ACB, BAC, BCA, CAB, or CBA.

PRACTICE | Use the diagram below to answer the questions that follow.

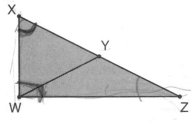

13. Every triangle can be named six ways. Two ways to name the largest triangle in the diagram above are WXZ and WZX. What are the other four ways?

13. ZWX   XWZ
    WZX   XZW

14. Triangle WXZ is the largest triangle in the diagram above. Name the two smaller triangles in the diagram.

14. XWY   WYZ

15. Which of the three triangles in the diagram above is a right triangle?

15. XWZ

16. Which of the three triangles in the diagram above is an acute triangle?

16. WXY

17. Which of the three triangles in the diagram above is an obtuse triangle?

17. WYZ

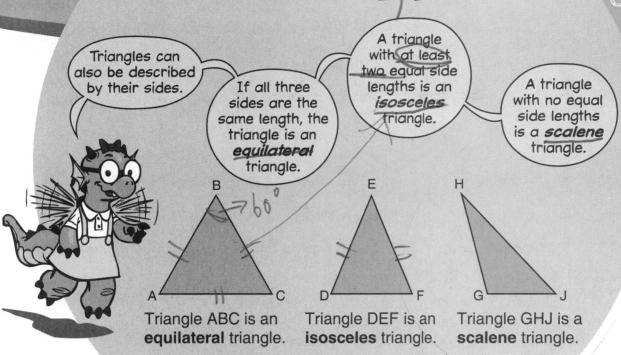

7 = 2

A+B+C = 180

→60°

Triangle ABC is an **equilateral** triangle.

Triangle DEF is an **isosceles** triangle.

Triangle GHJ is a **scalene** triangle.

PRACTICE | Use the diagram below to answer the questions that follow.

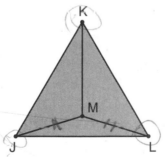

18. There are four different triangles in the diagram above.
    Name them all.

18. JKL MLJ
    KLM KMJ

19. Name the only equilateral triangle in the diagram above.

19. JKL

20. Name the two scalene triangles in the diagram above.

20. KLM KMJ

21. There are two isosceles triangles in the diagram above. Name them
    both. (Remember, a triangle with *at least* two equal side lengths is
    isosceles.)

21. MLJ KLJ

PRACTICE Draw a line to connect each of the descriptions below to one of the drawings on the right. If a shape is impossible, connect it to the circle marked "Impossible".

22. An isosceles right triangle.

23. A scalene obtuse triangle.

24. An isosceles obtuse triangle.

25. A scalene right triangle.

26. An equilateral right triangle.

27. A scalene acute triangle.

Impossible

PRACTICE | In the diagram below, RTUV is a square.
Use the diagram to answer the questions that follow.

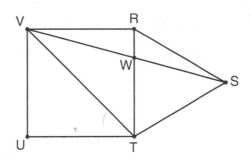

28. How many right triangles are in the diagram above?

28. _____3_____

29. Describe triangle TUV by its sides (equilateral, isosceles, or scalene) and by its angles (acute, right, or obtuse).

29. __*right*__ __*isosceles*__

30. Describe triangle RST by its sides (equilateral, isosceles, or scalene) and by its angles (acute, right, or obtuse).

30. _____

31. Describe triangle STW by its sides (equilateral, isosceles, or scalene) and by its angles (acute, right, or obtuse).

31. _____

32. Name the only scalene right triangle in the diagram above.

32. _____

33. Name the only isosceles obtuse triangle in the diagram above.

33. _____

34. ★ Name all three scalene obtuse triangles in the diagram above.

34. _____

When counting the number of triangles in a diagram, it helps to be organized.

First, find out how many different sizes of triangles there are. Then, count how many triangles there are of each size.

EXAMPLE

How many triangles of any size can be traced in the diagram below?

There are 8 small triangles,

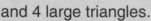
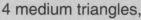

4 medium triangles,

and 4 large triangles.

So, there are a total of 8 + 4 + 4 = **16** triangles.

PRACTICE | Count the total number of triangles of any size that can be traced in each of the diagrams below.

35.

36.

$6 + 2 + 2 = 12$
$6 + 2 =$

37. ★

38. ★

$8 + 1 + 2 + 2$
$2 + 2 = 17$

35. _10_

36. _8_

37. _12_

38. _17_

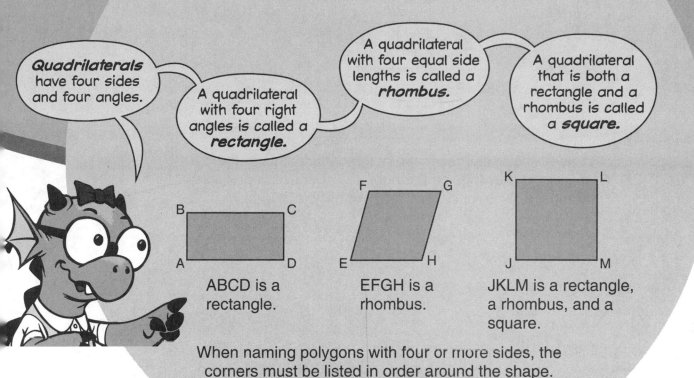

Quadrilaterals have four sides and four angles.

A quadrilateral with four right angles is called a **rectangle.**

A quadrilateral with four equal side lengths is called a **rhombus.**

A quadrilateral that is both a rectangle and a rhombus is called a **square.**

ABCD is a rectangle.

EFGH is a rhombus.

JKLM is a rectangle, a rhombus, and a square.

When naming polygons with four or more sides, the corners must be listed in order around the shape. For example, rectangle ABCD above could be named BCDA, but **not** ABDC.

PRACTICE

39. Draw a square that has its corners on four of the points below.

40. Draw a rectangle that has its corners on four of the points below.

41. Draw a rhombus that has its corners on four of the points below.

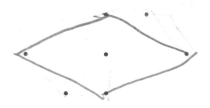

42. ★ Draw a quadrilateral that has its corners on four of the points below.

PRACTICE | Draw a line to connect each of the descriptions below to one of the drawings on the right. If a shape is impossible, connect it to the circle marked "Impossible".

43. A rectangle that is not a square.

44. A quadrilateral with exactly one right angle.

45. A rhombus.

46. A quadrilateral with exactly two right angles.

47. A quadrilateral that has four acute angles.

48. A quadrilateral that can be cut into two acute triangles.

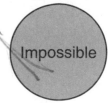

Impossible

EXAMPLE

If you answer "false" for any of the questions below, draw a shape that shows that the statement is false.

True or False:
If you cut a square into two identical pieces, the pieces will always be triangles or rectangles.

This statement is **false**.
It is possible to cut a square into two identical pieces that are not triangles or rectangles.

PRACTICE | Mark each statement below either true or false. For each false answer, draw a shape that shows that the statement is false.

49. **All** squares are rectangles.

49. _____

50. **All** rhombuses are squares.

50. _____

51. **Every** quadrilateral can be cut between two corners into two identical triangles.

51. _____

52. **Any** two identical triangles can be attached to make a quadrilateral.

52. _____

53. **Any** quadrilateral can be split into two smaller quadrilaterals by a straight line from the middle of one side to the middle of another side.

53. _____

Counting squares, rectangles, and rhombuses can be tricky.

EXAMPLE | How many different squares have all four corners on points in the grid below?

You can make these squares:
four small squares,   one big square, and one medium square.

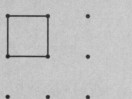 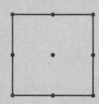 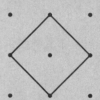

There are a total of $4+1+1=6$ squares.
Watch out for tricky shapes in the problems below.

PRACTICE | Answer each shape-counting question below.

54. How many different **rhombuses** have all four corners on points in the grid below?

54.  3

55. How many different **rectangles** have all four corners on points in the grid below?

55.  9

56. How many different **squares** have all four corners on points in the
★ grid below?

 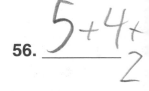

57. How many different **rhombuses** have all four corners on points in the
★ grid below?

57. _____

58. How many different **rectangles** have all four corners on points in the
★ grid below?
★

58. _____

Shapes with more than four sides have names, too!

Five sides: Pentagon

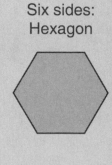

Six sides: Hexagon

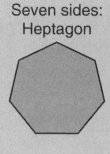

Seven sides: Heptagon

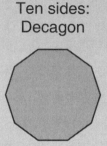

Eight sides: Octagon

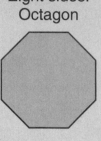

Nine sides: Nonagon

Ten sides: Decagon

The shapes above are all *regular*. A shape is regular if all its sides and angles are the same. Not all polygons are regular.

PRACTICE | Label each shape below as a pentagon, hexagon, heptagon, octagon, nonagon, or decagon.

59.

60.

61.

62.

63.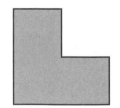

64.

59. _____

60. _____

61. _____

62. _____

63. _____

64. _____

Beast Academy Practice 3A

PRACTICE | Answer the questions about diagonals below.

65. All quadrilaterals have two diagonals.
Draw the two diagonals for each quadrilateral below.

66. All pentagons have the same number of diagonals.
How many diagonals does a pentagon have?

66.

67. All hexagons have the same number of diagonals.
How many diagonals does a hexagon have?

67.

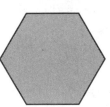

68. ★ A heptagon has 14 diagonals, and an octagon has 20. Look for a pattern in the number of diagonals of a quadrilateral, pentagon, hexagon, heptagon, and octagon. Continue the pattern to guess the number of diagonals of a nonagon.

68. _____

Making your own game cards is a great way to learn about new shapes!

Materials:
Timer, game cards, drawing paper, and pencils. Sample cards are on the next page. You can print these cards and more at BeastAcademy.com, or make your own.

Players:
4 or more, divided into two teams.

Object:
Describe the shapes given on the game cards so that your teammates can draw them. You cannot say the words listed below each shape, or any of the words in the name of the shape.

Game Play:
Players divide into two teams. Team A chooses a player to be the clue-giver. The clue-giver gets the deck of cards.

The clue-giver from team A has one minute to describe as many shapes from the deck as possible without using any of the forbidden words on the card. Players from team A try to draw the shape being described by their clue-giver. Players from Team B sit so that they can see the cards.

The clue-giver is only allowed to use words. No gestures are allowed (for example, tracing the shape in the air or making it with your hands). The clue-giver may not use any part or form of the forbidden words (if "triangle" is forbidden, then so is "angle"). "Sounds like" and "rhymes with" clues are also not allowed.

Scoring:
If a player from team A correctly draws the shape described by their clue-giver, team A gets the card. If team B catches the clue-giver from team A using one of the forbidden words on the card, team B gets the card. Teams take turns choosing a clue-giver until everyone has had a turn, or until all the cards have been used. The team with the most cards at the end of the game wins.

Judging:
Drawings do not need to be identical to what is on the card. For example, if the card has △, and a player draws ◿, or any other isosceles right triangle, it counts. If the card has a ▱, credit is given for any rhombus.

Isosceles Right Triangle

You can't say:

Triangle (or angle)
Three
Isosceles
Right

Five-Pointed Star

You can't say:

Five
Point
Star
Decagon

Square

You can't say:

Quadrilateral
Four
Equal
Right

Circle

You can't say:

Circle
Round
Curve
Center

Regular Pentagon

You can't say:

Pentagon
Five
Equal
Sides

Rhombus

You can't say:

Quadrilateral
Four
Equal
Diamond

Crescent

You can't say:

Moon
Circle
Overlap
Round

The Letter M

You can't say:

M
Angle
Four
W

Equilateral Triangle

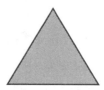

You can't say:

Triangle (or angle)
Three
Equilateral (or equal)
Sides

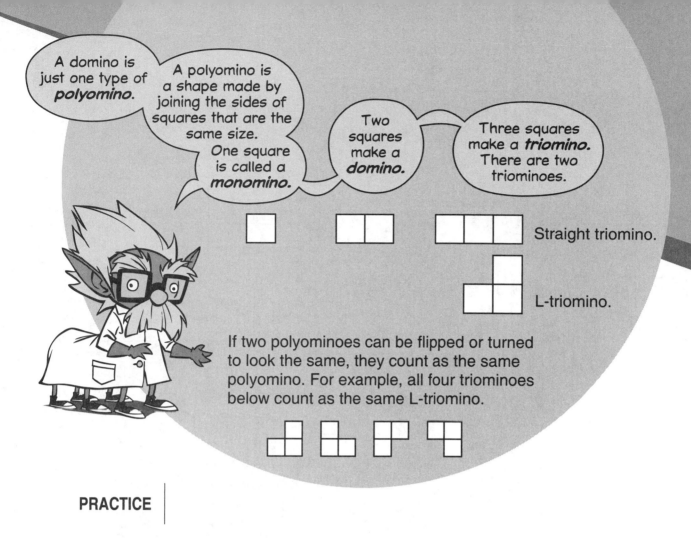

A domino is just one type of *polyomino.*

A polyomino is a shape made by joining the sides of squares that are the same size. One square is called a *monomino.*

Two squares make a *domino.*

Three squares make a *triomino.* There are two triominoes.

Straight triomino.

L-triomino.

If two polyominoes can be flipped or turned to look the same, they count as the same polyomino. For example, all four triominoes below count as the same L-triomino.

PRACTICE

69. Four squares make a tetromino. There are a total of five different tetrominoes. One has been traced for you on the grid below. Trace the other four tetrominoes.

Remember that if you can flip or turn one to look like another, they count as the same tetromino.

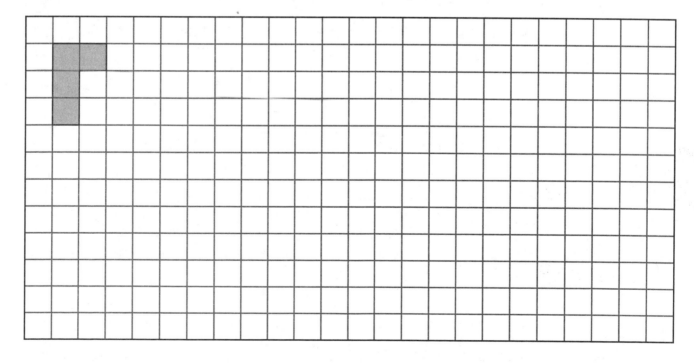

EXAMPLE

How can five dominoes be arranged to create the shape below?

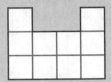

Many shapes can be created by fitting polyominoes together like a puzzle.

There is only one way to arrange five dominoes to make the shape:

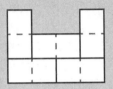

You can cut out the polyominoes on the facing page to use for the puzzles in this section, or print a page of polyominoes to cut out at BeastAcademy.com.

PRACTICE

70. Arrange eight L-triominoes to create this shape with a hole in the middle.

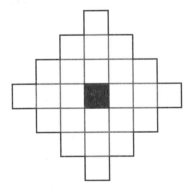

71. Arrange one monomino, one L-triomino, and four straight triominoes to make a square.

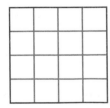

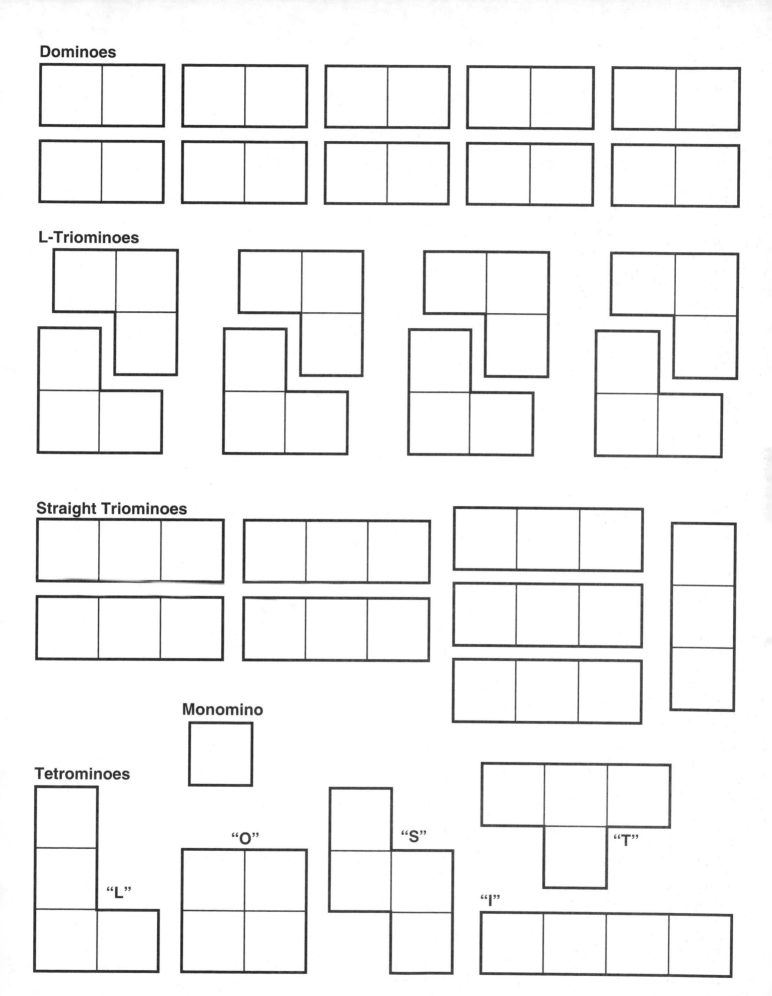

Dominoes

L-Triominoes

Straight Triominoes

Monomino

Tetrominoes

"L" "O" "S" "T"

"I"

PRACTICE | Arrange the five tetrominoes (one of each) to create each of the shapes below. Problems 72–75 are from the Lab section beginning on page 34 of the Guide.

72. ★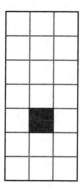

73. ★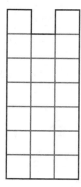

74. ★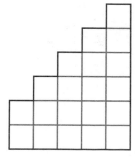

75. ★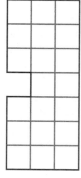

76. ★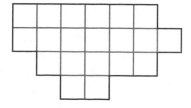

77. ★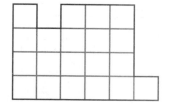

Some shapes are impossible to make with dominoes.

EXAMPLE

A hexomino is made by joining six squares. How many of the hexominoes below are **impossible** to make with three dominoes?

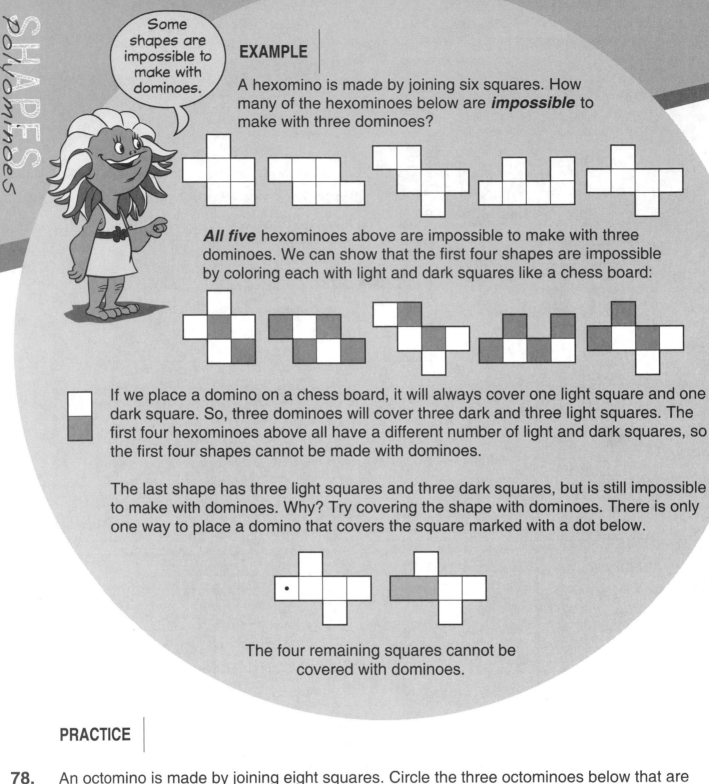

All five hexominoes above are impossible to make with three dominoes. We can show that the first four shapes are impossible by coloring each with light and dark squares like a chess board:

If we place a domino on a chess board, it will always cover one light square and one dark square. So, three dominoes will cover three dark and three light squares. The first four hexominoes above all have a different number of light and dark squares, so the first four shapes cannot be made with dominoes.

The last shape has three light squares and three dark squares, but is still impossible to make with dominoes. Why? Try covering the shape with dominoes. There is only one way to place a domino that covers the square marked with a dot below.

The four remaining squares cannot be covered with dominoes.

PRACTICE

78. An octomino is made by joining eight squares. Circle the three octominoes below that are **impossible** to make with dominoes.

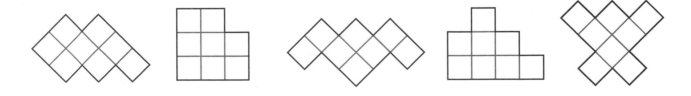

79. Each square below has a hole in it. Circle the shape that is **impossible** to make with 12 dominoes.

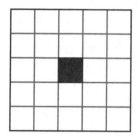 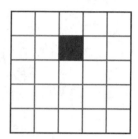 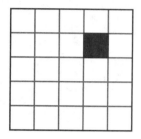

80. ★ Circle the only shape below that **can be made** with one T-tetromino (⬛) and four dominoes.

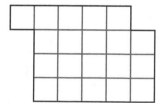 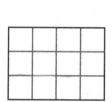 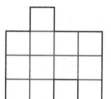 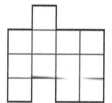 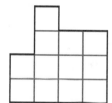 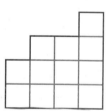

81. ★★ Circle the shape below that is **impossible** to make with the five tetrominoes (one of each):

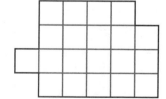 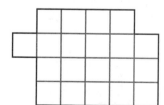

Challenge: Make the two shapes that are possible with the five tetrominoes.

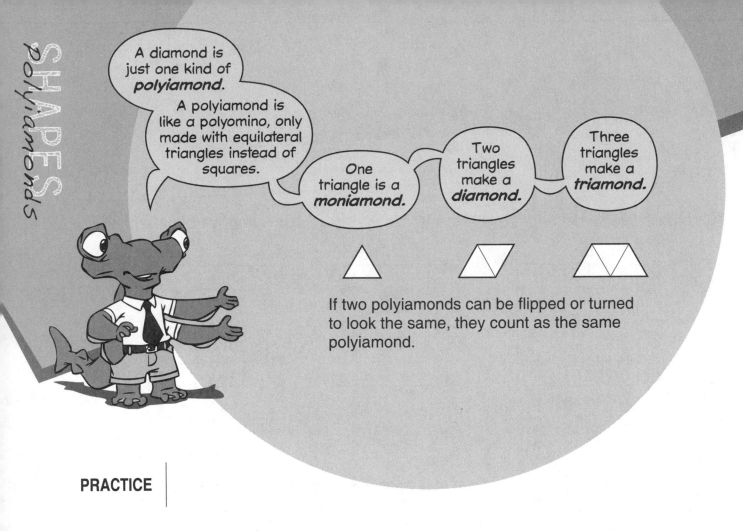

A diamond is just one kind of **polyiamond**.

A polyiamond is like a polyomino, only made with equilateral triangles instead of squares.

One triangle is a **moniamond**.

Two triangles make a **diamond**.

Three triangles make a **triamond**.

If two polyiamonds can be flipped or turned to look the same, they count as the same polyiamond.

PRACTICE

82. There are a total of three different polyiamonds that can be made from four equilateral triangles. They are called tetriamonds. Trace the three tetriamonds on the grid below.

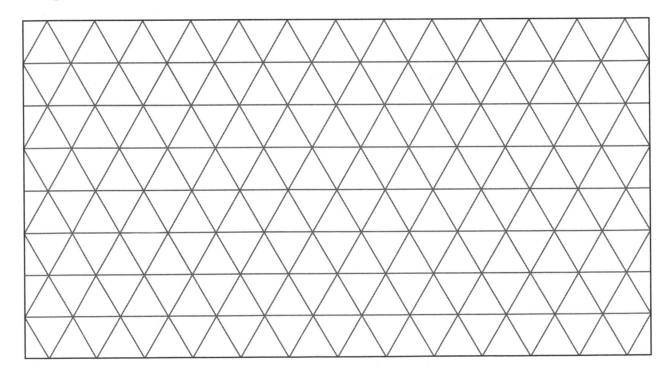

83. There are a total of four different polyiamonds that can be made from five equilateral triangles. They are called pentiamonds. Trace the four pentiamonds on the grid below.
Remember that if you can flip or turn one to look like another, they count as the same pentiamond.

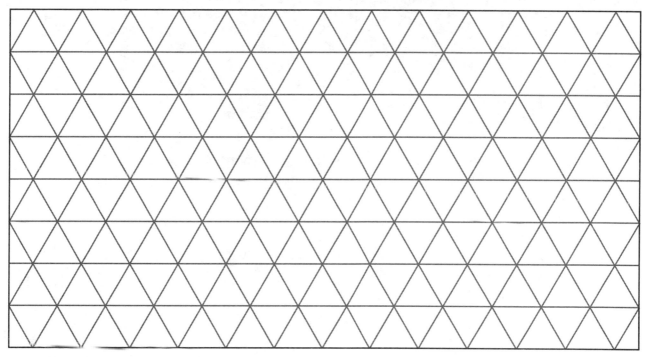

84. Look at the outlines of the three tetriamonds you drew on the previous page.
How many of these are:

Triangles? _____

Quadrilaterals? _____

Pentagons? _____

Hexagons? _____

85. Look at the four pentiamonds you drew above.
How many of these are:

Triangles? _____

Quadrilaterals? _____

Pentagons? _____

Hexagons? _____

Heptagons? _____

PRACTICE | Solve each of the toothpick arrangement puzzles below.
Draw your final arrangement in the space below each puzzle.

86. Six toothpicks can be arranged as shown to make two triangles. How can only five toothpicks be arranged to make two triangles?

87. Nine toothpicks can be arranged as shown to make four triangles. How can nine toothpicks be arranged to make five triangles? (The triangles do not all need to be the same size.)

88. Ten toothpicks can be arranged as shown to make three rhombuses. How can only nine toothpicks be arranged to make three rhombuses?

89.
★ Seven toothpicks can be arranged to make two squares. How can six toothpicks be arranged to make five squares? (The squares do not all need to be the same size.)

EXAMPLE | Move three toothpicks in the arrangement below to leave three squares.

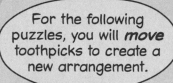

For the following puzzles, you will **move** toothpicks to create a new arrangement.

One solution is shown. The new arrangement has three squares.

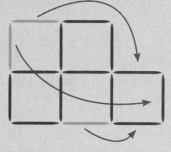

For all of the toothpick puzzles, every toothpick should be part of a shape in the new arrangement. For example, the attempt below leaves three squares, but the toothpick marked with an X is not part of a square, so this is not a correct solution.

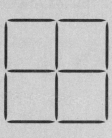

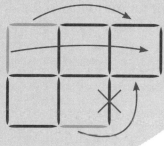

PRACTICE | Begin each toothpick puzzle below with the given arrangement.

90. Move two toothpicks to make two equilateral triangles.

91. Move four toothpicks to make two squares.

It is sometimes useful to consider what the final toothpick arrangement will look like.

For example, if you have 7 toothpicks to make 2 squares, the squares must share a side.

But, if you have 8 toothpicks to make 2 squares, the squares cannot share a side.

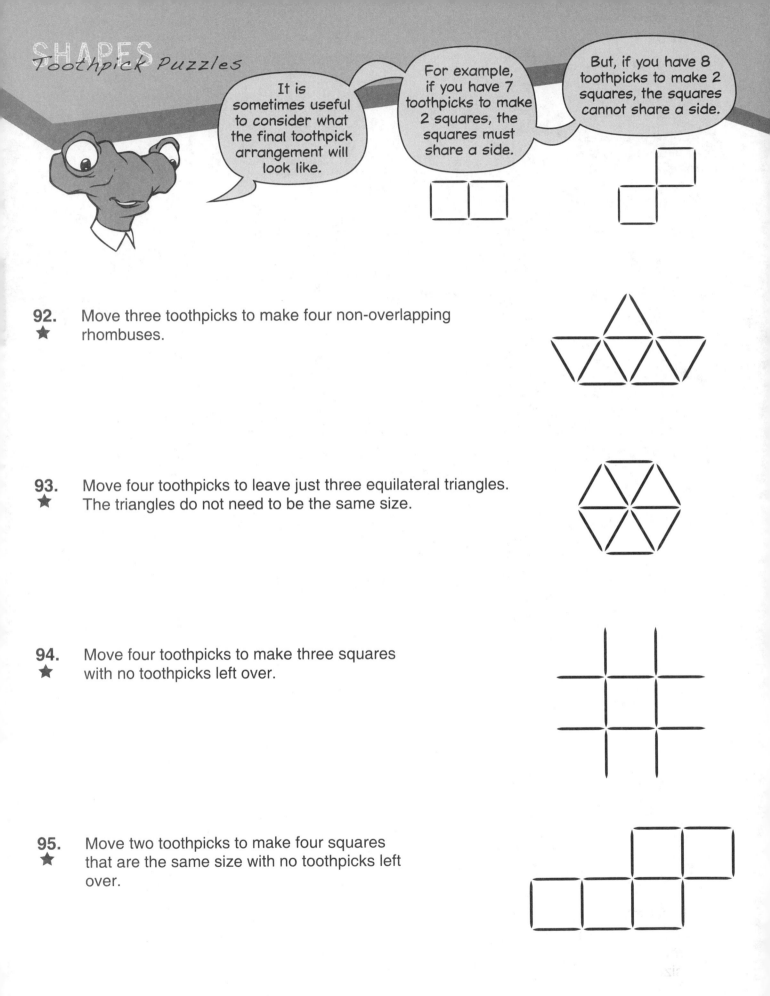

92. ★ Move three toothpicks to make four non-overlapping rhombuses.

93. ★ Move four toothpicks to leave just three equilateral triangles. The triangles do not need to be the same size.

94. ★ Move four toothpicks to make three squares with no toothpicks left over.

95. ★ Move two toothpicks to make four squares that are the same size with no toothpicks left over.

Careful! In the toothpick puzzles below, you are **removing** toothpicks, not moving them.

PRACTICE | For the toothpick puzzles below, you are **removing** toothpicks.

96. There are five squares in the arrangement shown (four small and one large). Remove two toothpicks to leave just two squares.

97. How many equilateral triangles are there in this arrangement?

97. _____

98. Remove three toothpicks to leave just three equilateral triangles.

99. How many squares are there in this arrangement?

99. _____

100. Remove four toothpicks to leave just five squares.

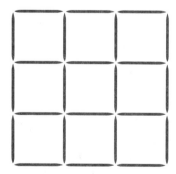

101. How many equilateral triangles are there in this arrangement?

101. _____

102. What is the smallest number of toothpicks that ★ must be removed so that no triangles of any ★ size are left in the diagram?

102. _____

CHAPTER 2
Skip-Counting

Use this Practice book with Guide 3A.

Recommended Sequence:

Book	Pages:
Guide:	42–49
Practice:	39–44
Guide:	50–55
Practice:	45–58
Guide:	56–65
Practice:	59–63

You may also read the entire chapter in the Guide before beginning the Practice chapter.

When we **skip-count,** we add the same number over and over again.

EXAMPLE | Skip-count by 4's to 28.

We begin at 4, and then add 4 over and over to get to 28.

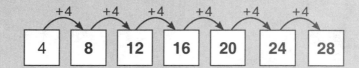

| 4 | 8 | 12 | 16 | 20 | 24 | 28 |

PRACTICE

1. Skip-count by 2's to 20.

| 2 | 4 | 6 | 8 | 10 | 12 | 14 | 16 | 18 | 20 |

2. Skip-count by 5's to 50.

| 5 | 10 | 15 | 20 | 25 | 30 | 35 | 40 | 45 | 50 |

3. Skip-count by 3's to 30.

| 3 | 6 | 9 | 12 | 15 | 18 | 21 | 24 | 27 | 30 |

4. Skip-count by 10's to 100.

| 10 | 20 | 30 | 40 | 50 | 60 | 70 | 80 | 90 | 100 |

5. Skip-count by 11's to 110.

| 11 | 22 | 33 | 44 | 55 | 66 | 77 | 88 | 99 | 110 |

Skip-counting helps us count objects more quickly.

Instead of counting each of these jellybeans one by one, I can skip-count by 5's. There are:

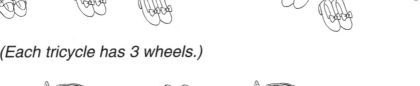

5 · +5 · 10 · +5 · 15 · +5 · **20** jellybeans.

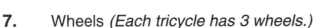

PRACTICE | Count the number of each given object in the pictures below.

6. Shoes

6. _____

7. Wheels *(Each tricycle has 3 wheels.)*

7. _____

8. Pigeons

8. _____

9. Legs *(Each slumberbee has 6 legs.)*

9. _____

10. Legs *(Each octapug has 8 legs.)*

10. _____

Beast Academy Practice 3A

PRACTICE | Count the number of each given object in the pictures below.

11. Flower petals *(Each flower has 9 petals.)*

11. _____

12. Total number of sides *(Each shape below is a decagon.)*

12. _____

13. Spikes *(Each porcupod has 15 spikes.)*

13. _____

    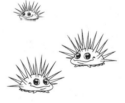

14. Spots *(Each spotted jackalope has 50 spots.)*

14. _____

15. Each coin below is worth 25 cents. How many cents are the coins worth all together?

15. _____

Grogg made all of the following patterns using gumballs.

EXAMPLE | How many gumballs did Grogg use to make the pattern below?

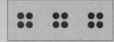

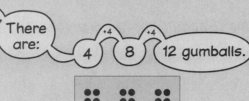

There are: 4 +4 8 +4 12 gumballs.

Grogg used **12** gumballs to make the pattern.

PRACTICE | Find the number of gumballs that Grogg used to make each pattern.

16.

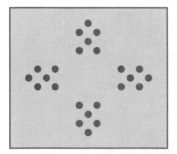

16. _____

17.

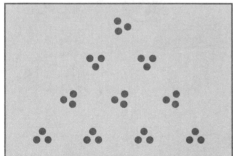

17. _____

18.

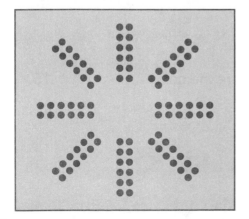

18. _____

PRACTICE | Find the number of gumballs that Grogg used to make each pattern.

19.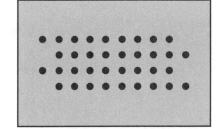

19. _____

20.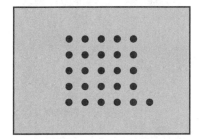

20. _____

21.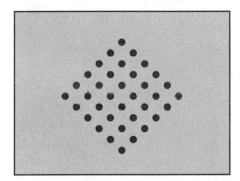

21. _____

22.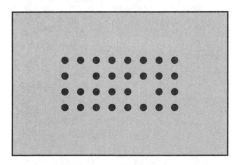

22. _____

23.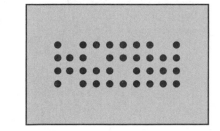

23. _____

PRACTICE | Find the number of gumballs that Grogg used to make each pattern.

24.

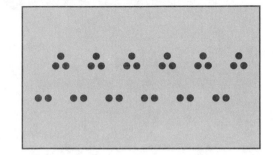

24. _____

25.

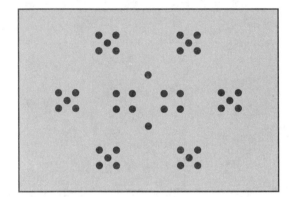

25. _____

26.

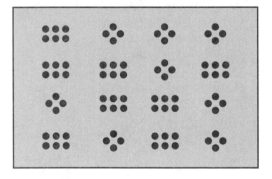

26. _____

27.

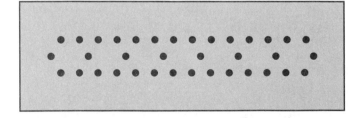

27. _____

28.

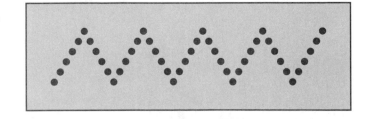

28. _____

The numbers we say when we skip-count by a number are **multiples** of that number.

For example, the numbers we use to skip-count by 11 are 11, 22, 33, 44, and so on. These are all multiples of 11.

Look for patterns as you mark multiples of numbers in the hundred charts below.

You can print more hundred charts at BeastAcademy.com.

PRACTICE | Use the hundred chart below to answer the questions that follow.

1	2	3	4	5	6	7	8	9	10
11	12	13	14	15	16	17	18	19	20
21	22	23	24	25	26	27	28	29	30
31	32	33	34	35	36	37	38	39	40
41	42	43	44	45	46	47	48	49	50
51	52	53	54	55	56	57	58	59	60
61	62	63	64	65	66	67	68	69	70
71	72	73	74	75	76	77	78	79	80
81	82	83	84	85	86	87	88	89	90
91	92	93	94	95	96	97	98	99	100

29. Mark all multiples of 2 with a ◻.
How many numbers in the 100 chart are multiples of 2?

29. _____

30. Mark all multiples of 5 with a ◿.
How many numbers in the 100 chart are multiples of 5?

30. _____

31. Numbers that are multiples of both 2 and 5 are marked above with a ⊠. List the ten numbers from the 100 chart that are multiples of both 2 and 5.

32. Complete this statement:
The numbers that are multiples of both 2 and 5 are the multiples of _____.

33. How many numbers in the 100 chart are **not** a multiple of 2 or of 5?

33. _____

PRACTICE | Use the hundred chart below to answer the questions that follow.

1	2	3	4	5	6	7	8	9	10
11	12	13	14	15	16	17	18	19	20
21	22	23	24	25	26	27	28	29	30
31	32	33	34	35	36	37	38	39	40
41	42	43	44	45	46	47	48	49	50
51	52	53	54	55	56	57	58	59	60
61	62	63	64	65	66	67	68	69	70
71	72	73	74	75	76	77	78	79	80
81	82	83	84	85	86	87	88	89	90
91	92	93	94	95	96	97	98	99	100

34. Mark all multiples of 8 with a ◻.
How many numbers in the 100 chart are multiples of 8?

34. _____

35. Mark all multiples of 3 with a ◹.
How many numbers in the 100 chart are multiples of 3?

35. _____

36. Numbers that are multiples of both 8 and 3 are marked above with a ⊠. Name the four numbers in the 100 chart that are multiples of both 8 and 3.

36. _____ _____

_____ _____

37. What is the smallest number over 100 that is a multiple of both 8 and 3?

37. _____

38. Complete this statement:
The numbers that are multiples of both 8 and 3 are the multiples of _____.

38. _____

PRACTICE | Use the hundred chart below to answer the questions that follow.

1	2	3	4	5	6	7	8	9	10
11	12	13	14	15	16	17	18	19	20
21	22	23	24	25	26	27	28	29	30
31	32	33	34	35	36	37	38	39	40
41	42	43	44	45	46	47	48	49	50
51	52	53	54	55	56	57	58	59	60
61	62	63	64	65	66	67	68	69	70
71	72	73	74	75	76	77	78	79	80
81	82	83	84	85	86	87	88	89	90
91	92	93	94	95	96	97	98	99	100

39. Mark all multiples of 4 with a ◁.
How many numbers in the 100 chart are multiples of 4?

39. _____

40. Mark all multiples of 6 with a ◿.
How many numbers in the 100 chart are multiples of 6?

40. _____

41. Numbers that are multiples of both 4 and 6 are marked above with a ⊠. How many numbers in the 100 chart are multiples of both 4 and 6?

41. _____

42. Complete this statement:
The numbers that are multiples of both 4 and 6 are the multiples of _____.

42. _____

43. What number in the hundred chart is a multiple of 4, 6, and also *5*?

43. _____

PRACTICE | Use the clues below and your work on the previous pages to figure out each little monster's number.

44. When Cammie colors the multiples of a number in her 100 chart, she colors exactly 10 numbers. What is Cammie's number?

44. _____

45. When Lizzie colors the multiples of a number in her 100 chart, she colors exactly 33 numbers, including 18, 33, and 90. What is Lizzie's number?

45. _____

46. When Ralph colors the multiples of a number in his 100 chart, he colors exactly two numbers in the 30's. He also colors 42. What is Ralph's number?

46. _____

47. When Alex colors the multiples of a number in his 100 chart, he colors exactly two numbers in the 20's, two numbers in the 30's, and two numbers in the 40's. What is Alex's number?

47. _____

48.
★ When Winnie colors the multiples of a number in her 100 chart, she colors in exactly 8 numbers. What is Winnie's number?

48. _____

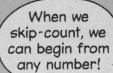

When we skip-count, we can begin from any number!

For example, we can skip-count by 5's, beginning at 3:

EXAMPLE | Continue the pattern below.

3, 8, 13, 18, __, __, __, __, __, __, __, ...

+5 +5 +5 +5 +5 +5 +5 +5 +5

3, 8, 13, 18, **23**, **28**, **33**, **38**, **43**, **48**, ...

PRACTICE | Fill in the blanks to continue each pattern below.

49. 1, 3, 5, 7, _____, _____, _____, _____, _____, _____, ...

50. 9, 17, 25, 33, _____, _____, _____, _____, _____, _____, ...

51. 4, 7, 10, 13, _____, _____, _____, _____, _____, _____, ...

52. 3, 7, 11, 15, _____, _____, _____, _____, _____, _____, ...

53. 5, 14, 23, 32, _____, _____, _____, _____, _____, _____, ...

54. 29, 36, 43, 50, _____, _____, _____, _____, _____, _____, ...

55. 98, 103, 108, 113, _____, _____, _____, _____, _____, _____, ...

PRACTICE | Some of the numbers in the patterns below have already been filled in. Complete each pattern.

56. 4, 8, _____, _____, _____, _____, 28, 32, _____, _____, ...

57. 5, _____, _____, _____, _____, _____, 35, 40, _____, _____, ...

58. _____, 12, 18, _____, _____, _____, 42, _____, ...

59. 73, _____, _____, _____, 81, 83, _____, _____, _____, ...

60. 5, 9, _____, _____, _____, _____, 29, _____, _____, ...

61. ★ _____, _____, 21, _____, _____, _____, 49, _____, 63, ...

62. ★ _____, _____, _____, 32, _____, _____, 56, _____, 72, ...

63. ★★ _____, 10, _____, _____, _____, 26, _____, _____, 38, ...

64. ★★ _____, _____, 36, _____, _____, 51, _____, _____, _____, 71, ...

In the mazes below, begin at the shaded number. Follow a skip-counting pattern to escape.
You may only move up, down, left, or right to the next number.

EXAMPLE | Escape this maze.

18	8	25	19
11	5	9	13
17	12	48	14
23	29	16	8

We begin at the shaded square and escape at the exit marked below the 29. We can move up, down, left or right.

If we move left to 11, we can continue skip-counting by 6's to escape the maze:

18	8	25	19
11	5	9	13
17	12	48	14
23	29	16	8

5, 11, 17, 23, 29, ...

This is our escape path!

If we had moved right to 9, we would have tried to continue skip-counting by 4's to escape the maze:

5, 9, 13, 17, ...

No square above, below, or beside 13 contains the number 17.

18	8	25	19
11	5	9	13
17	12	48	14
23	29	16	8

> Watch out for tricky dead ends!

PRACTICE | Begin at the shaded number and escape each maze below.
There is only one escape path for each maze. Watch out for dead ends!

65.

20	30	21	3	18
16	23	28	33	38
13	18	11	15	17
8	3	6	14	16
7	4	9	12	14

66.

35	37	45	53	61
21	13	24	35	69
5	16	56	46	77
21	79	68	57	85
101	90	43	62	90

67.

24	20	25	5	18
23	16	9	2	10
42	38	11	6	26
52	34	16	10	14
15	30	26	22	18

68.

10	12	14	15	18
8	6	9	12	21
4	7	14	25	24
2	8	17	30	27
12	9	15	33	32

SKIP-COUNTING
Maze Escape

PRACTICE | Begin at the shaded number and escape each maze below.
There is only one escape path for each maze. Watch out for dead ends!

69.

52	91	13	22	31
52	15	4	28	36
63	26	12	20	44
84	76	68	60	52
25	17	82	25	16

70.

90	5	86	50	31
104	95	42	73	27
92	86	13	17	21
68	77	9	5	14
59	50	41	32	23

71.

52	37	47	28	64
22	27	57	53	57
21	17	20	49	71
25	53	14	45	52
29	33	37	41	47

72.

22	15	21	27	33
16	9	13	76	18
23	18	15	23	43
30	37	44	33	50
14	26	51	58	35

73.

15	90	15	27	34	41
70	80	30	20	24	48
60	50	40	22	28	32
65	60	56	52	39	36
31	64	68	48	44	40
51	76	72	85	56	42

74.

127	135	143	151	159	175
119	59	71	83	167	179
111	47	36	95	155	143
103	35	23	107	119	131
95	82	31	39	47	142
87	79	71	63	55	73

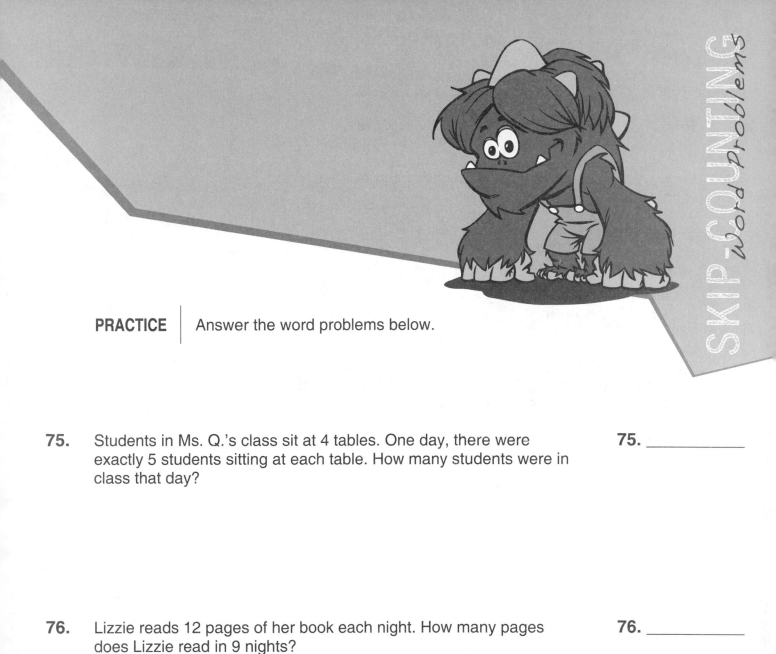

PRACTICE | Answer the word problems below.

75. Students in Ms. Q.'s class sit at 4 tables. One day, there were exactly 5 students sitting at each table. How many students were in class that day?

75. _____

76. Lizzie reads 12 pages of her book each night. How many pages does Lizzie read in 9 nights?

76. _____

77. How many sides do 111 triangles have all together?

77. _____

PRACTICE | Answer the word problems below.

78. Grogg skip-counts by 100's. The first number he says is 100. What is the 17th number he says?

78. _____

79. Alex skip-counts by 12's. The first number he says is 12. What is the 1,000th number he says?

79. _____

80. Lizzie skip-counts by 6's. The first number she says is 6. What is the 20th number she says?

80. _____

81. What is the 50th number in the pattern below?

7, 14, 21, 28, ...

81. _____

PRACTICE | Answer the word problems below.

82. Winnie begins skip-counting at 54. She skip-counts higher than 70, but never says the number 70. Which of the numbers below could Winnie be skip-counting by?

82. _____

2   4   6   8   16

83. Ralph begins skip-counting at 5. He skip-counts higher than 35, but never says the number 35. Which of the numbers below could Ralph be skip-counting by?

83. _____

2   3   4   5   30

84. Cammie begins skip-counting at 23. While skip-counting, she says the number 68. Which of these numbers is Cammie definitely *not* skip-counting by?

84. _____

2   3   5   9   15

85. Grogg begins skip-counting at 9. While skip-counting, he says the number 65. Which of these numbers is Grogg definitely *not* skip-counting by?

85. _____

2   4   7   8   9

PRACTICE | Answer the word problems below.

86. Lizzie begins at 10 and skip-counts by 10's. Winnie begins at 6 and skip-counts by 6's. What is the smallest number that Winnie and Lizzie both say?

86. _____

10, _____, _____, _____, _____, _____, _____, _____, _____, _____

6, _____, _____, _____, _____, _____, _____, _____, _____, _____

87. Winnie begins at 9 and skip-counts by 9's. Grogg begins at 4 and skip-counts by 4's. What is the smallest number that Winnie and Grogg both say?

87. _____

9, _____, _____, _____, _____, _____, _____, _____, _____, _____

4, _____, _____, _____, _____, _____, _____, _____, _____, _____

88. Grogg begins at 2 and skip-counts by 8's. Alex begins at 2 and skip-counts by 3's. What is the smallest number after 2 that Grogg and Alex both say?

88. _____

2, _____, _____, _____, _____, _____, _____, _____, _____, _____

2, _____, _____, _____, _____, _____, _____, _____, _____, _____

89. Alex begins at 4 and skip-counts by 7's. Lizzie starts at 4 and skip-counts by 6's. What is smallest number after 4 that Alex and Lizzie both say?

89. _____

4, _____, _____, _____, _____, _____, _____, _____, _____, _____

4, _____, _____, _____, _____, _____, _____, _____, _____, _____

PRACTICE | Answer the word problems below.

90. Winnie begins at 6 and skip-counts by 3's. Alex starts at 3 and skip-counts by 8's. What is the smallest number that Winnie and Alex both say?

90. _____

6, ____, ____, ____, ____, ____, ____, ____, ____, ____, ____

3, ____, ____, ____, ____, ____, ____, ____, ____, ____, ____

91. Cammie begins at 5 and skip-counts by 5's. Lizzie starts at 0 and skip-counts by a number less than 10. The first number that Cammie and Lizzie both say is 15. What is the only number that Lizzie could be skip-counting by?

91. _____

92. There are between 50 and 60 students in the Beast Academy choir. When the choir stands in rows of 8, there is one extra member. How many students are in the Beast Academy choir?

92. _____

93. Between 70 and 100 monsters will attend the Beast Academy Talent
★ Show. If seated in rows of 7, there will be 1 extra monster. If seated
in rows of 11, there will be no extra monsters. How many monsters
will attend the talent show?

93. _____

94. What is the 11th number in the pattern below?
★

$$8, 14, 20, ...$$

94. _____

95. What is the 101st number in the pattern below?
★
★

$$5, 14, 23, 32, 41, ...$$

95. _____

We can find an object's weight with a balance scale.

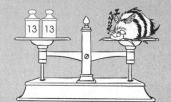

The slumberbee is balanced with two 13-gram weights.

So, this slumberbee weighs
$13 + 13 = $ **26 grams**.

PRACTICE

96. Alex balances an elefinch with fifteen 7-gram weights. What is the weight of the elefinch?

96. _____

97. Grogg balances a 60-gram pandakeet using only 5-gram weights. How many weights does he use?

97. _____

98. Ralph balances a 85-gram pandakeet using only 5-gram weights. How many weights does he use?

98. _____

99. Lizzie balances a 27-gram octapug using only 3-gram weights. How many weights does she use?

99. _____

100. How many ***more*** 3-gram weights will Lizzie need to balance a 66-gram octapug than she needs to balance a 45-gram octapug?

100. _____

PRACTICE

101. Can you balance 15 grams using only 3-gram weights?
✎ If so, how many would you need? If not, why not?

102. Can you balance 27 grams using only 4-gram weights?
✎ If so, how many would you need? If not, why not?

103. How many weights would you need to balance 18 grams using only 8-gram weights and 5-gram weights?

103. _____

104. How many weights would you need to balance 39 grams using only 11-gram and 7-gram weights?

104. _____

105. What is the *smallest* number of weights you could use to balance 40 grams using only 4-gram and 9-gram weights?

105. _____

106. What is the *smallest* number of weights you would need to balance 44 grams using only 3-gram and 7-gram weights?

106. _____

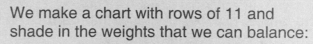

EXAMPLE

What is the largest number of grams that **cannot** be balanced with only 6-gram and 11-gram weights?

Using a chart with rows of 11 makes it easier to find all the weights we can balance.

We make a chart with rows of 11 and shade in the weights that we can balance:

1	2	3	4	5	6	7	8	9	10	11
12	13	14	15	16	17	18	19	20	21	22
23	24	25	26	27	28	29	30	31	32	33
34	35	36	37	38	39	40	41	42	43	44
45	46	47	48	49	50	51	52	53	54	55
56	57	58	59	60	61	62	63	64	65	66

The largest weight we cannot balance is **49 grams**.

PRACTICE

107. How many different weights **cannot** be balanced with only 2-gram and 13-gram weights?

107. _____

1	2	3	4	5	6	7	8	9	10	11	12	13
14	15	16	17	18	19	20	21	22	23	24	25	26
27	28	29	30	31	32	33	34	35	36	37	38	39
40	41	42	43	44	45	46	47	48	49	50	51	52

108. What is the largest number of grams that **cannot** be balanced with only 3-gram and 7-gram weights?

108. _____

1	2	3	4	5	6	7
8	9	10	11	12	13	14
15	16	17	18	19	20	21
22	23	24	25	26	27	28
29	30	31	32	33	34	35

In the problems below, it may help to draw a chart like those on the previous page.

109. What is the largest number of grams that **cannot** be balanced with
★   only 5-gram and 7-gram weights?

109. _____

110. What is the largest number of grams that **cannot** be balanced with
★   only 4-gram and 9-gram weights?

110. _____

111. What is the largest number of grams that ***cannot*** be balanced with
★   only 3-gram and 8-gram weights?

111. _____

112. Is there a largest number of grams that cannot be balanced with only
★   4-gram and 6-gram weights? If so, what is it? If not, explain why not.
✏

CHAPTER 3
Perimeter & Area

Use this Practice book with Guide 3A.

Recommended Sequence:

You may also read the entire chapter in the Guide before beginning the Practice chapter.

Perimeter is the distance around the outside of a shape.

To find the perimeter of any polygon, add the lengths of its sides.

EXAMPLE | Find the perimeter of the triangle below.

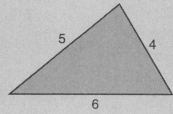

5   4

6

$4+6+5 = 15.$

The perimeter of the triangle is **15**.

PRACTICE | Find the perimeter of each polygon below.

1.

11   9

12

1. __32__

2.

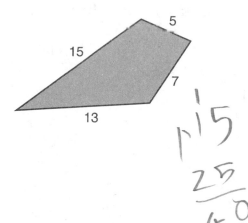

5

15

7

13

$\begin{array}{r} 15 \\ 25 \\ \hline 40 \end{array}$

2. __40__

3.

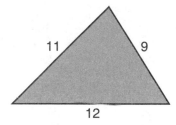

14

8

12

$\begin{array}{r} 20 \\ 14 \\ \hline 34 \end{array}$

3. __34__

4.

8

6   12

14

4. __40__

The sides of a **regular polygon** are all the same length.

If you know the side length of a regular polygon, you can find its perimeter.

PRACTICE

5. Label the remaining sides of the regular pentagon below.

4

4

4

4

4

6. What is the perimeter of the pentagon above?

6. ___20___

Find the perimeter of each regular shape below.

7. Square

6

6

6

6

7. ___24___

8. Nonagon

3 3
3
3
3
3
3
3
3

$6 \times 4 = 24$

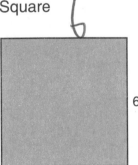

8. ___27___

9. What is the perimeter of a regular pentagon with sides of length 7?

$5 \times 7 = 35$

9. ___35___

10. ★ What is the length of each side of a regular hexagon whose perimeter is 60?

$6 \times 60 = 360$

10. ___360___

Beast Academy Practice 3A

Opposite sides of a rectangle are the same length.

If we know the height and width of a rectangle, we can find its perimeter!

PRACTICE

11. Label the remaining sides of the rectangle below.

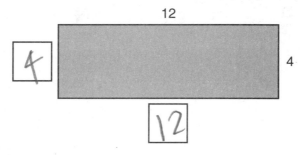

12

4

4

12

12. What is the perimeter of the rectangle above?

12. ___32___

Find the perimeter of each rectangle below.

13.

7

13

13

14.

16

8

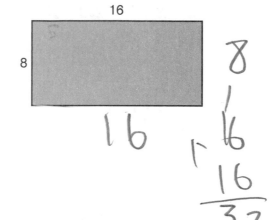

8

16

16

16
___
32

+32
16
___
48

13. ___40___

14. ___48___

15. Is it possible to draw a rectangle that has whole-number side lengths and a perimeter of 13? If it is possible, draw one. If it isn't possible, explain why.

it iseht possible becuse 13 iseht eveh.

A shape is **rectilinear** if its sides always meet at right angles.

Sometimes, we can find the missing side lengths of a rectilinear shape using the opposite sides.

EXAMPLE | Find the missing side length of the rectilinear shape below.

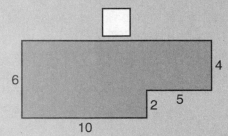

We can find the width by adding the lengths of the two horizontal sides at the bottom of the shape.

$$10+5 = 15.$$

The missing side length is **15**.

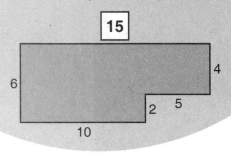

PRACTICE

16. Label the missing side lengths of the rectilinear shape below.

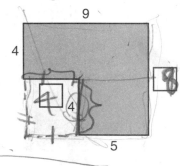

17. What is the perimeter of the shape above?

17. ___34___

18. Find the perimeter of the rectilinear shape below.
★

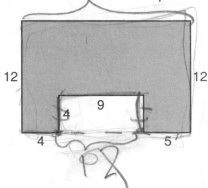

18. ___68___

Beast Academy Practice 3A

EXAMPLE | Find the perimeter of the rectilinear shape below.

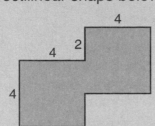

> Sometimes, we can find the perimeter of a rectilinear shape without finding the lengths of all of its sides.

The two horizontal sides on top add up to $4+4=8$, so the two horizontal sides on the bottom must also add up to 8.

The two sides on the left add up to $2+4=6$, so the two sides on the right must also add up to 6.

The perimeter of the shape is the same as a 6 by 8 rectangle:

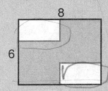

$6+8+6+8=(6+8)+(6+8)=14+14=28$.
The perimeter of the shape is **28**.

PRACTICE | Find the perimeter of each rectilinear shape below.

19.

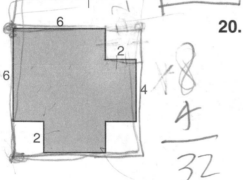

19. ___32___

20.

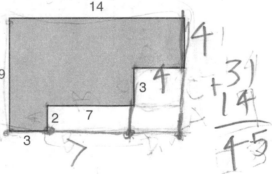

20. ___46___

21.

21. ___52___

22. ★ ✏️ Can you find the perimeter of the rectilinear shape below? If not, can you explain why it's impossible?

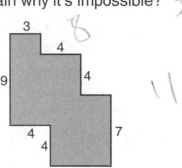

PERIMETER & AREA

Review

PRACTICE | Find the perimeter of each shape labeled below.

23. Rectangle

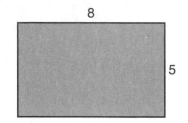

8

5

24. Regular Hexagon

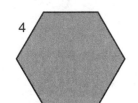

4

25. Pentagon

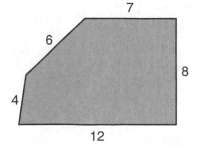

7

6

8

4

12

26. Nonagon

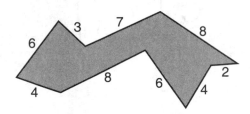

3   7   8

6   2

4   8   6   4

27. Octagon

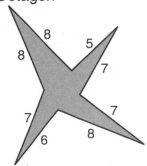

8   5

8   7

7   7

6   8

28.
★ Rectilinear Octagon

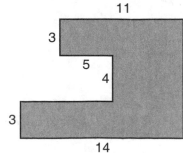

11

3

5

4

3

14

23. _____

24. _____

25. _____

26. _____

27. _____

28. _____

29. Alex, Grogg, and Winnie draw polygons that look like the first letters of their names. Which polygon has the greatest perimeter?

29. _____

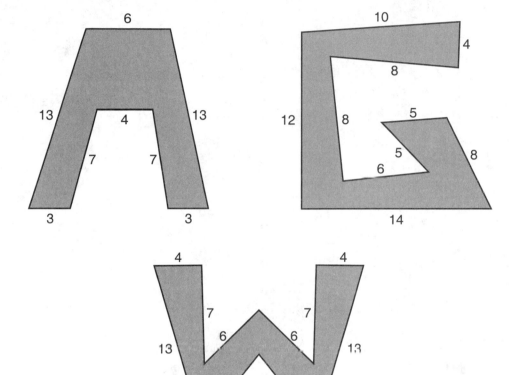

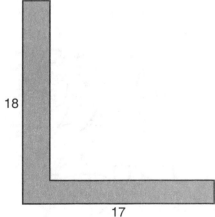

30. Lizzie draws a rectilinear "L". How does the perimeter of her shape compare to the perimeters of Alex's, Grogg's, and Winnie's shapes above?

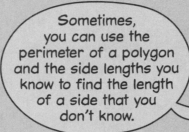

Sometimes, you can use the perimeter of a polygon and the side lengths you know to find the length of a side that you don't know.

EXAMPLE | Find the missing side length of the triangle below, which has a perimeter of 23.

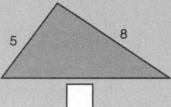

$(5+8)+\boxed{}=23.$

$13+\boxed{}=23.$

$23-13=10,$ so $13+\boxed{10}=23.$

The missing side length is **10**.

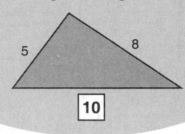

PRACTICE | Use the given perimeter and side lengths to label the missing side length for each of the following polygons.

31. Perimeter = 51.

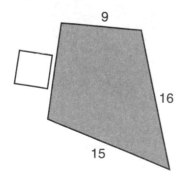

32. Perimeter = 50.

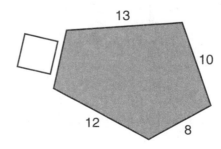

33. Perimeter = 42.

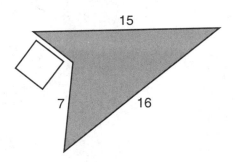

34. Perimeter = 49.

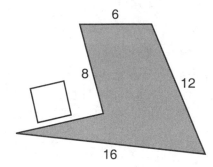

35. Perimeter = 55.

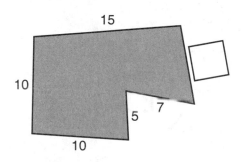

36. Perimeter = 60.

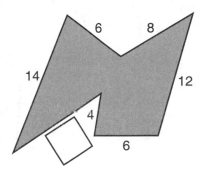

37. The rectangle below has a perimeter of 50. What is its height?

37.

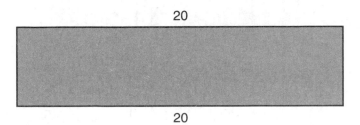

PRACTICE

38. What is the perimeter of a hexagon that has two sides of length 1, one side of length 3, two sides of length 4, and one side of length 5?

38. _____

39. Winnie arranges five sticks to make a pentagon that has a perimeter of 16 inches. If four of the sticks are 3 inches long, what is the length of the fifth stick?

39. _____

Each small square in the grids below has side length 1.
Use the grids to answer the questions.

40. Trace a rectilinear shape with a perimeter of 36 on the grid below.

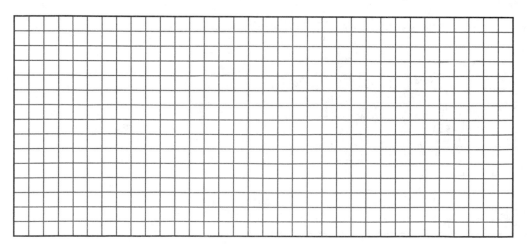

41. Trace a rectangle on the grid below that has a perimeter of 20 and a width of 7.

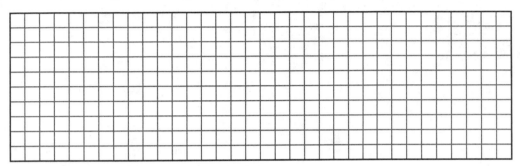

42. How many rectangles with different heights can you draw on the grid below such that each rectangle has a perimeter of 16?

42.

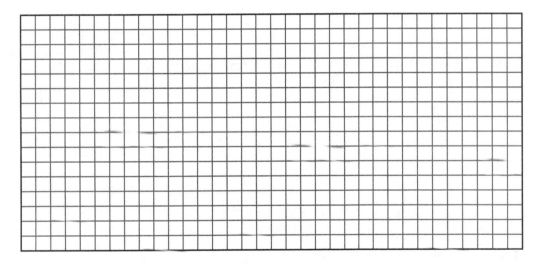

43. Trace a rectangle on the grid below whose width is 5 more than its height and whose perimeter is between 15 and 20.

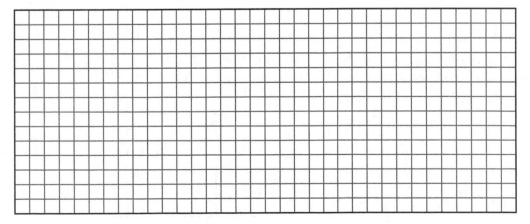

44. The shapes below are rectilinear.
Circle the two shapes that have the same perimeter.

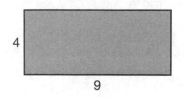

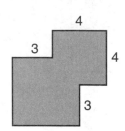

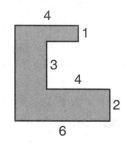

45. Alex's rectangle has a perimeter of 18 inches. Lizzie's rectangle has the same width but is one inch taller than Alex's rectangle. What is the perimeter of Lizzie's rectangle?

45. _____

46. Winnie's rectangle has a perimeter of 26 inches. Grogg's rectangle is three inches taller and one inch wider than Winnie's. What is the perimeter of Grogg's rectangle?

46. _____

47. ★ If you increase the width of a rectangle by 5 inches, you get a rectangle with a perimeter of 22 inches. What is the perimeter of the ***original*** rectangle?

47. _____

48. The square below has side length 12.
Grogg cuts the square along the dotted line to make two
congruent rectangles. What is the perimeter of one of these
rectangles?

48. _____

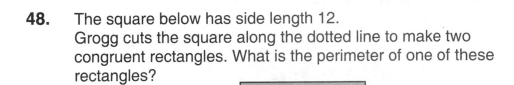

49. The square below has a perimeter of 40.
★ Grogg cuts the square as shown to make four congruent squares.
What is the perimeter of one of these small squares?

49. _____

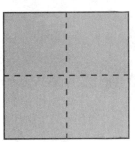

50. Grogg cuts the square below into two congruent rectangles.
★ Each rectangle has a perimeter of 24.
★ What is the perimeter of the original square?

50. _____

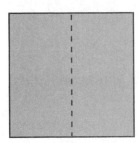

PRACTICE |

51. Two regular heptagons with side length 1 are attached as shown. What is the perimeter of the shape they create?

51. _____

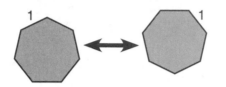 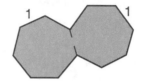 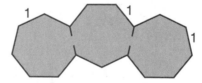

52. Grogg suggests for Problem 51, "The new shape is made from two heptagons. To find its perimeter, we can just double the perimeter of one heptagon." Why doesn't this work?

53. A third heptagon is attached as shown. What is the perimeter of the new shape?

53. _____

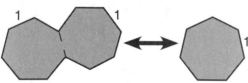

54. We attach a fourth regular heptagon to the end of our 3-heptagon shape above. How much **greater** is the perimeter of the 4-heptagon shape than the perimeter of the 3-heptagon shape?

54. _____

55. Eight regular heptagons with side length 1 are attached in the same way that we attached the heptagons in the problems above. What is the perimeter of the shape they create?
★
★

55. _____

EXAMPLE

Three squares are attached as shown. Each square has a perimeter of 3. What is the perimeter of the L-shape they make?

In these problems, we don't need to know the length of each side to find the perimeter of the shape.

Each square has 4 sides. The perimeter of the L-shape is made of 8 sides of these squares.

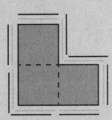

So, we can double the perimeter of the square to find the perimeter of the L-shape. Since the perimeter of each square is 3, the perimeter of the L-shape is 3+3 = **6**.

PRACTICE

56. Four equilateral triangles are arranged as shown. Each triangle has a perimeter of 4. What is the perimeter of the quadrilateral they make?

56.

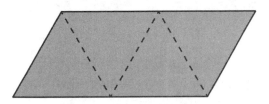

57. Three regular hexagons are arranged as shown. Each hexagon has a perimeter of 8. What is the perimeter of the larger shape they make?

57.

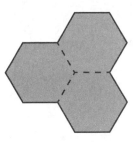

58. Six regular hexagons are arranged as shown. The perimeter of each hexagon is 5. What is the perimeter of the shape they make?

58.

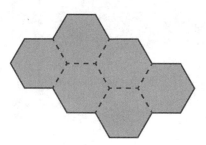

59. Five squares are arranged as shown. Each square has a perimeter of 7. What is the perimeter of the shape they make?

59.

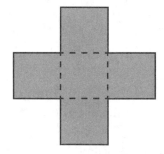

60. Six regular pentagons are arranged as shown. Each pentagon has a perimeter of 12. What is the perimeter of the shape they make?

60.

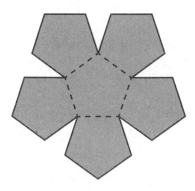

PRACTICE

Use the following for Problems 61 and 62:
Grogg and Alex live 7 miles from each other.
Alex lives 5 miles from the park.

61. What is the greatest possible distance from Grogg's house to the park?

61. _____

62. What is the shortest possible distance from Grogg's house to the park?

62. _____

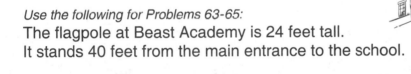

Use the following for Problems 63-65:
The flagpole at Beast Academy is 24 feet tall.
It stands 40 feet from the main entrance to the school.

63. If the flagpole falls, what is the closest that the top of the pole could land from the school entrance?

63. _____

64. If the flagpole falls, what is the farthest that the top of the pole could land from the school entrance?

64. _____

65. After the flagpole falls, which of the following **could** be the distance from the top of the flagpole to the school entrance?
(You may circle more than one.)

10 feet   30 feet   50 feet   70 feet

The Triangle Inequality

The lengths of the two short sides of a triangle must add up to more than the length of the long side. This is called the Triangle Inequality.

Any three numbers that satisfy the Triangle Inequality can be used as the side lengths of a triangle.

PRACTICE | *Use the following for the problems below:*
Captain Kraken's pirate ship has a triangular flag. One side of the triangle is 4 feet long, and another side is 7 feet long.

66. Fill in the blanks:

The third side of Kraken's flag must be longer than
_____ feet but shorter than _____ feet.

67. Which of the following **could** be the length of the third side of Kraken's flag? (You may circle more than one.)

2 feet   4 feet   6 feet   8 feet   10 feet   12 feet

68. Which of the following **could** be the perimeter of Kraken's flag? (You may circle more than one.)

13 feet   16 feet   19 feet   22 feet   24 feet   25 feet

69. Each pole below is labeled with its length. Circle the groups of three poles that can be attached at the ends to form a triangle.

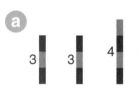

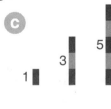

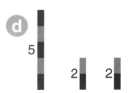

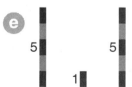

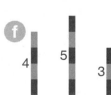

70. What is the perimeter of an isosceles triangle with sides of
★ length 3 and 7?

70. _____

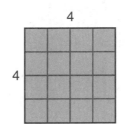

Area is the amount of space a shape takes up.

To find the area of a rectangle, split it into small squares and count the number of squares.

PRACTICE | Find the area of each rectangle.

71.
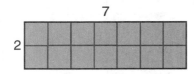
7
2

71. 14

72.
4
4

72. 16

73.
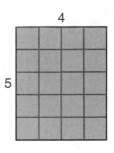
4
5

73. 20

74.
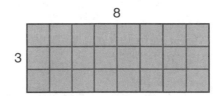
8
3

74. 24

75.
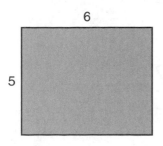
6
5

75. 36

76.
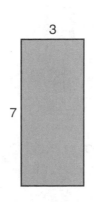
3
7

76. 21

To find the area of a rectilinear shape, you can split the shape into rectangles and add the areas of the rectangles.

EXAMPLE | Find the area of the rectilinear shape below.

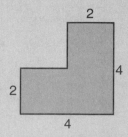

2
4
2
4

To find the area of this shape, we can split it into two rectangles like this:

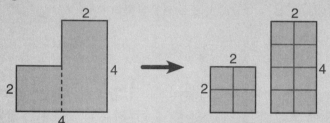

Then we add the areas of the rectangles: 4+8 = 12.
The area of the shape is **12 squares**.

PRACTICE | Find the area of each rectilinear shape.

77.

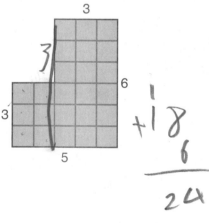

3
3
6
3
5

+18
6
24

78.

2
2
5
3

10   15.   +10
13
25

79.

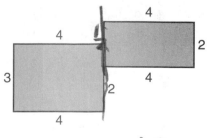

4
4
3
2
4
2
4

12

+8
2
12
26

80.

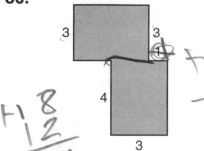

4
3
3
4
3

+12
12
24

84

PERIMETER & AREA
Rectilinear Shapes

81.

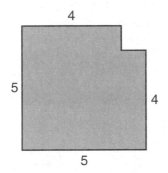

82.

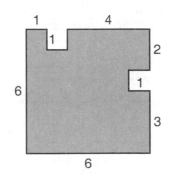

83.

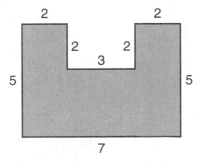

84.

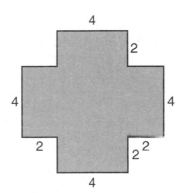

85.
★

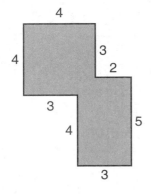

86.
★
★

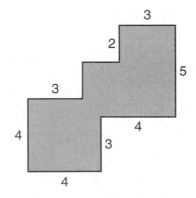

81. _____

82. _____

83. _____

84. _____

85. _____

86. _____

PRACTICE | Each small square in the grids below has side length 1.
You may use the grids to help answer the questions.

87. The perimeter of a square is 20. What is its area?

87. _____

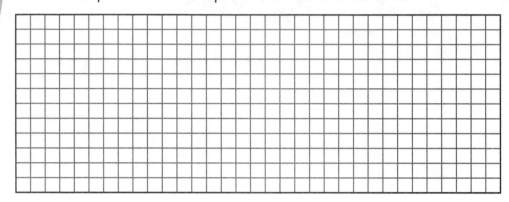

88. What is the area of a rectangle that has a width of 7 and a perimeter of 18?

88. _____

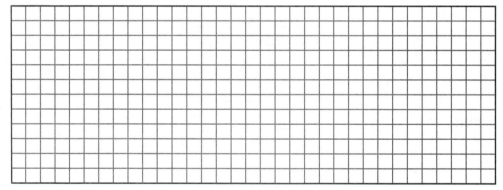

89. A rectangle covers an area of 11 squares.
The length of each side of the rectangle is a whole number.
What is the perimeter of this rectangle?

89. _____

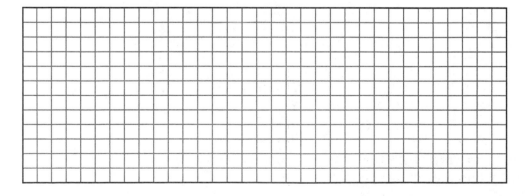

Alex has drawn all of the rectangles with whole-number side lengths and area equal to 12 squares. Use this diagram for the problems below.

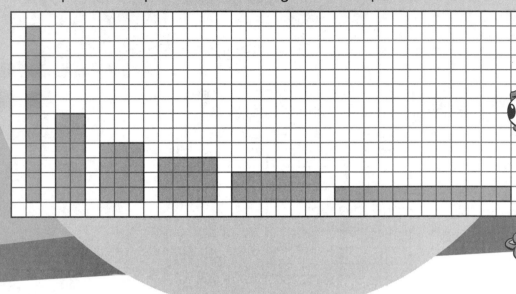

90. What is the **largest** possible perimeter of a rectangle that has whole-number side lengths and an area of 12 squares?

90. _____

91. What is the **smallest** possible perimeter of a rectangle that has whole-number side lengths and an area of 12 squares?

91. _____

Next, Alex wants to compare the rectangles that have whole-number side lengths and a perimeter of 12.

92. ★ Use the grid below to trace all of the rectangles that have whole-number side lengths and a **perimeter** of 12.

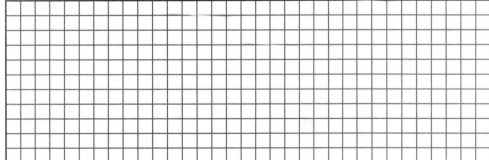

93. What is the **largest** possible area of a rectangle that has whole-number side lengths and a perimeter of 12?

93. _____

94. What is the **smallest** possible area of a rectangle that has whole-number side lengths and a perimeter of 12?

94. _____

PRACTICE | Winnie is tracing rectilinear shapes on a grid.
Below is one shape she traced.

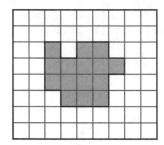

95.   What is the perimeter of Winnie's shape above?   95. _____

96.   What is the area of Winnie's shape?   96. _____

97.   On the diagram below, shade the square that can be added to Winnie's
★   shape that would **decrease** its perimeter.

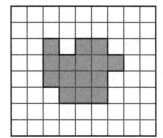

98.   Winnie wants to add one square to her shape **without** changing its
★   perimeter. Shade a square that she could add.
       (There are three possible answers. Can you find them all?)

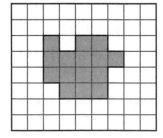

Beast Academy Practice 3A

99. Trace a rectangle on the grid below that has the same **area** as Winnie's shape. Is the **perimeter** of your rectangle larger, smaller, or the same as the perimeter of Winnie's shape?

99. _____

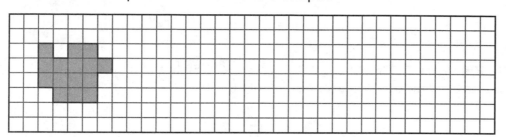

100. ★ Trace a rectangle on the grid below that has a **larger area** and a **smaller perimeter** than Winnie's shape.

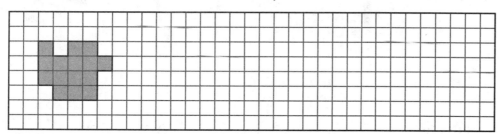

Challenge: Find the rectangle with the largest area whose perimeter is smaller than Winnie's.

101. ★ Trace a rectangle on the grid below that has a **larger perimeter** and a **smaller area** than Winnie's shape.

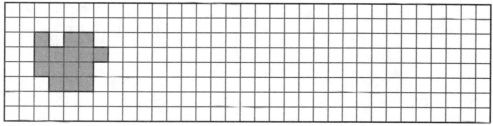

Challenge: Find the rectangle with the largest perimeter whose area is smaller than Winnie's.

PRACTICE | Review the problems on the previous two pages. Then, state whether each statement below is true or false.

102. Two shapes that have the same perimeter always have the same area.

102. _____

103. Given two shapes, the one with the larger area always has a larger perimeter.

103. _____

104. Given two shapes, the one with the larger perimeter always has a larger area.

104. _____

PRACTICE

105. ★ Grogg cuts along the dashed lines in the square below to split it into four congruent squares. The perimeter of each smaller square is 12. What is the **area** of the larger square?

105. _____

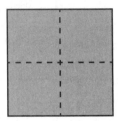

Each small square in the grids below has side length 1.
You may use the grids to help answer the questions.

106. ★★ Rectangles with areas of 3, 10, and 12 squares can be arranged to form a square. What is the perimeter of this square?

106. _____

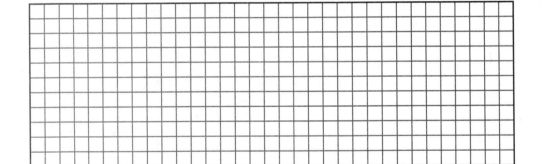

107. ★★ A rectilinear shape has 12 sides. Each side has length 2. What is the area of this rectilinear shape?

107. _____

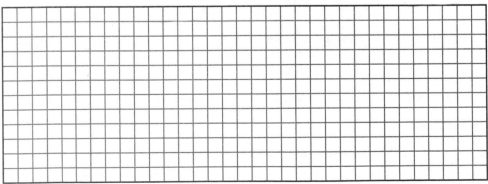

Grogg is cutting polygons out of other shapes. Grogg always cuts along the dashed lines. He makes two kinds of cuts: **straight cuts** and **squiggle cuts**.

The dashed lines separate the shapes into small squares with side length 1.

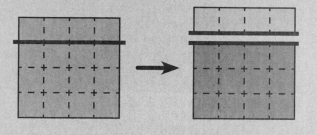

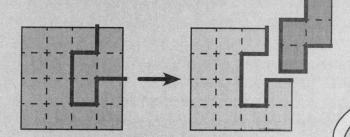

This **straight cut** splits the 4 by 4 square into two rectangles with a total perimeter of 10+14=24.

A **squiggle cut** follows the dashed lines but doesn't have to be straight!

This squiggle cut splits the square into two polygons with a total perimeter of 10+20=30.

PRACTICE

108. Grogg splits the rectangle below into two rectangles with the straight cut shown. What is the **total perimeter** of the two smaller rectangles he creates?

108. _____

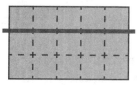

109. Grogg splits the rectangle below into two polygons with the squiggle cut shown. What is the **total perimeter** of the two polygons he creates?

109. _____

PRACTICE | The dashed lines split the shapes below into squares of side length 1.

Use this rectangle for questions 110 and 111.

110. If Grogg splits the rectangle into two rectangles with one **straight** cut, what is the **smallest** possible total perimeter of the two rectangles?

110. _____

You can experiment by drawing some possible cuts in these extra rectangles:

111. If Grogg splits the rectangle into two polygons with one **squiggle** cut, what is the **largest** possible total perimeter of the two polygons?

111. _____

You can experiment by drawing some possible cuts in these extra rectangles:

112. Grogg splits the shape below into two polygons with one **straight** cut.
★ Find all **four** possible values for the total perimeter of the polygons.

112. _____ _____

_____ _____

113. Using just one squiggle cut, Grogg can cut the shape below into two polygons that have
★ the same perimeter. Can you find a way to do this, too?
(There is more than one way, see if you can find them all.)

You can experiment by drawing some possible cuts in these extra shapes:

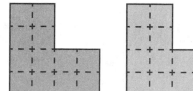

114. Grogg can cut the shape below into ***three*** polygons so that each has the same
★ perimeter. Figure out how this can be done. You can use straight and squiggle cuts.
(There is more than one way.)

You can experiment by drawing some possible cuts in these extra shapes:

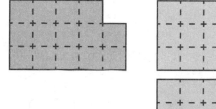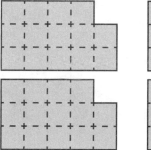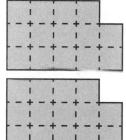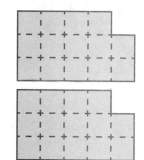

*Challenge: Figure out how to split the shape into **four** polygons with equal perimeter.*

115. Find a way to split the shape below into three polygons so that all three have the same
★ perimeter, but each has a different area. You can use straight and squiggle cuts.
★ *(There is more than one way.)*

You can experiment by drawing some possible cuts in these extra shapes:

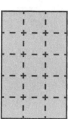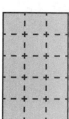

HINTS
For Selected Problems

Below are hints to every problem marked with a ★.
Work on the problems for a while before looking at the hints.
The hint numbers match the problem numbers.

CHAPTER 1
Shapes   6-37

11. Try to trace a path from start to finish. Then, try to trace a path backwards from finish to start. The paths should meet in the middle.

34. Two of the obtuse triangles have an obtuse angle at W. The third has its obtuse angle at T.

37. There are three different sizes.

38. There are four different sizes.

42. The point that is crossed out below is not a corner.

56. There are three different sizes.

57. All of the rhombuses are the same size, and there are more than three.

58. Look for rectangles that do not have horizontal and vertical sides, and remember that all squares are rectangles.

68. How many more diagonals does a pentagon have than a quadrilateral? How many more diagonals does a hexagon have than a pentagon?

72. Begin with the square "O" tetromino in a corner.

73. Begin with the long "I" tetromino filling one of the top squares.

74. Try working from top to bottom. There are seven ways to create this shape.

75. The long "I" tetromino shares at least one edge with each of the other four tetrominoes.

76. The long "I" tetromino must be placed horizontally to make this shape.

77. Begin by placing the "I" tetromino. Do you see why placements like the ones below cannot possibly work?

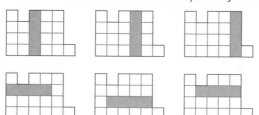

80. Color each board like a chess board. How many light and dark squares are on each? How many light and dark squares will a T-tetromino and four dominoes cover?

81. Color each board like a chess board. How many light and dark squares are on each? How many light and dark squares will the five tetrominoes cover? *Challenge Hint: Both shapes can be made with the I-tetromino in the top row.*

89. Try crossing two toothpicks.

92. Start by removing three toothpicks to leave three rhombuses.

93. One triangle will be larger than the other two.

94. There are 12 toothpicks. If twelve toothpicks make three squares, can any toothpick be a side of two squares?

95. There are 16 toothpicks. If 16 toothpicks make four squares, can any toothpick be a side of two squares?

102. Some toothpicks are part of more triangles than others. Each time you remove a toothpick, try to eliminate as many of the remaining triangles as possible.

CHAPTER 2
Skip-Counting   38-63

48. Is Winnie's number greater or less than 10?

61. We add some number twice to get from 49 to 63. $63 - 49 = 14$. What number are we skip-counting by?

62. We add some number twice to get from 56 to 72. $72 - 56 = 16$. What number are we skip-counting by?

63. We add some number *three* times to get from 26 to 38. $38 - 26 = 12$. What number are we skip-counting by?

64. We add some number *three* times to get from 36 to 51. $51 - 36 = 15$. What number are we skip-counting by?

93. The number of monsters who attended was one more than a multiple of 7, a multiple of 11, and is between 70 and 100.

94. Write out a few more numbers in the pattern. How many times do we add the number we are skip-counting by?

95. It may be helpful to write out a few more numbers in the pattern, but writing out all the numbers could take a long time! How many times will we add the number we are skip-counting by?

109. A chart can be most helpful if drawn with rows of 5 or 7, since these are the weights used in the problem.

110. A chart can be most helpful if drawn with rows of 4 or 9, since these are the weights used in the problem.

111. A chart can be most helpful if drawn with rows of 3 or 8, since these are the weights used in the problem.

112. A chart can be most helpful if drawn with rows of 4 or 6, since these are the weights used in the problem

CHAPTER 3
Perimeter and Area   64–93

10. A regular hexagon has 6 equal sides. What number can we add 6 times to get 60?

15. We can find the perimeter of a rectangle by *doubling* the sum of the rectangle's length and width.

18. Try adding the dashed line below to the diagram:

Remember that opposite sides of a rectangle are the same length.

22. We can create a rectangle with the same perimeter as the rectilinear shape.

Can we find the height and width of such a rectangle?

28. Try splitting the shape into rectangles. Here is one possible way:

Remember that opposite sides of a rectangle are the same length.

47. Increasing the width of a rectangle increases the length of *two* sides of the rectangle.

49. What is the side length of a square with perimeter 40? The side length of each smaller square is half the side length of the original square.

50. The height of each rectangle is the same length as the side of the original square. The width of each rectangle is half the side length of the original square. So, the width of each rectangle is half its height.

55. How much does the perimeter increase each time we attach another heptagon?

70. An isosceles triangle with sides of length 3 and 7 has either two sides of length 3 or two sides of length 7. Are both of these triangles possible to make?

85. Here is one way you may split up the shape.

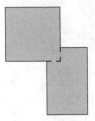

86. Here is one way you may split up the shape.

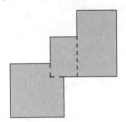

92. There are 5 different heights.

97. Where could we attach a square to the existing shape so that it will subtract more perimeter than it adds?

98. Where could we attach a square to the existing shape so that it will subtract exactly the same amount of perimeter as it adds?

100. Look back at #97. How did you increase the area but decrease the perimeter? Then, look at #98. Which squares can be added without changing the perimeter? Which squares can be added to make Winnie's shape a rectangle with a smaller perimeter?

101. It may be helpful to first think about how we could trace a shape with larger perimeter but the *same area* as Winnie's shape.

105. What is the side length of a square with perimeter 12?

106. What will the area of the square be?

107. Try a rectilinear shape that looks like a +.

112. What are the four possible lengths of straight cuts he could make?

113. Each of the two resulting pieces will have a perimeter that includes half of the boundary of the original shape.

114. Each polygon has a perimeter of 10.
Challenge Hint:
Each polygon has a perimeter of 8.

115. Each polygon has a perimeter of 10.

SOLUTIONS
Chapters 1-3

SHAPES
Angles   Page 7

1. We connect the points as shown.

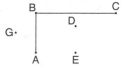

Angle ABC is a **right** angle.

2. We connect the points as shown.

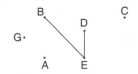

Angle DEB is an **acute** angle.

3. We connect the points as shown.

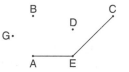

Angle AEC is an **obtuse** angle.

4. We connect the points as shown.

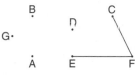

Angle CFE is an **acute** angle.

5. We connect the points as shown.

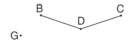

Angle BDC is an **obtuse** angle.

6. We connect the points as shown.

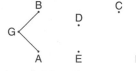

Angle BGA is a **right** angle.

SHAPES
Angle Mazes   8-9

7.

8.

9.

10.

11.

12.

SHAPES
Triangles   10-13

13. In addition to WXZ and WZX, the largest triangle can be named **XWZ**, **XZW**, **ZWX**, or **ZXW**.

14. The two smaller triangles are **WXY** and **WYZ**. Remember, the order of the letters is not important when naming triangles.

15. Triangle **WXZ** is a right triangle, with the right angle at W.

16. Triangle **WXY** is acute. All three of its angles are acute.

17. Triangle **WYZ** is an obtuse triangle, with the obtuse angle at Y.

18. The four triangles are **JLM**, **JKM**, **JKL**, and **KLM**.

19. Triangle **JKL** is equilateral.

20. Triangles **JKM and KLM** are scalene triangles.

21. Triangles **JLM and JKL** are isosceles triangles. Triangle JKL is also equilateral. Isosceles triangles have at least two equal side lengths. Since equilateral triangles have three equal side lengths, all equilateral triangles are isosceles.

22. An isosceles right triangle. (The arrow indicates the right angle.)

23. A scalene obtuse triangle.

24. An isosceles obtuse triangle.

25. A scalene right triangle.

26. An equilateral right triangle. (All equilateral triangles are acute.)

27. A scalene acute triangle.

Below, each description is connected to the correct shape for questions 22-27.

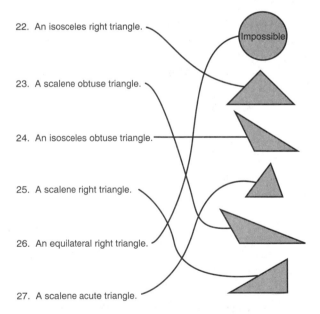

22. An isosceles right triangle.

23. A scalene obtuse triangle.

24. An isosceles obtuse triangle.

25. A scalene right triangle.

26. An equilateral right triangle.

27. A scalene acute triangle.

28. Since RTUV is a square, we know angles RVU, VUT, UTR, and TRV are all right angles. The triangles in the diagram that have one right angle are triangles TUV, RTV, and RVW.

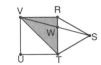

So, there are **3** right triangles in the diagram.

29. Triangle TUV has two sides of equal length (TU and UV) and a right angle at U. Therefore, triangle TUV is an **isosceles right** triangle.

30. Triangle RST is an **equilateral acute** triangle. Notice that all equilateral triangles are acute.

31. Triangle STW is a **scalene acute** triangle.

32. Triangle **RVW** is a scalene right triangle.

33. Triangle **RSV** is an isosceles obtuse triangle.

34. Triangles **TVW, RSW, and STV** are scalene obtuse triangles.

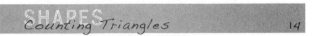

SHAPES
Counting Triangles   14

35. There are 8 small triangles and 2 large triangles.

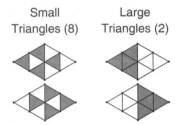

Small Triangles (8)   Large Triangles (2)

This makes a total of 8+2 = **10** triangles.

36. There are 5 small triangles and 5 large triangles.

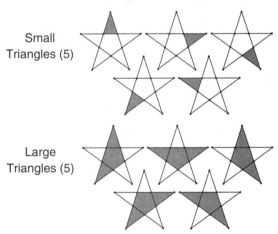

Small Triangles (5)

Large Triangles (5)

There are a total of 5+5 = **10** triangles.

37. There are 6 small triangles, 4 medium triangles, and 2 large triangles.

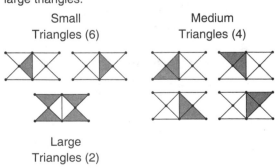

Small Triangles (6)   Medium Triangles (4)

Large Triangles (2)

There are a total of 6+4+2 = **12** triangles.

38. There are 8 small triangles, 6 medium triangles, 2 large triangles, and 1 giant triangle.

Small Triangles (8) Medium Triangles (6)

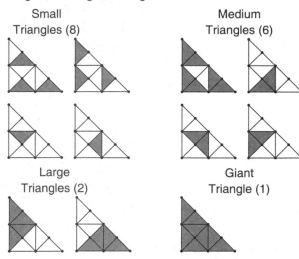

Large Triangles (2) Giant Triangle (1)

There are a total of 8+6+2+1 = **17** triangles.

SHAPES
Quadrilaterals   15-17

39. There is only one square that has its corners on four of the points, as shown below.

40. There is only one rectangle that has its corners on four of the points, as shown below.

41. There is only one rhombus that has its corners on four of the points, as shown below.

42. There are three different quadrilaterals that have their corners on four of the points, as shown below.

43. A rectangle that is not a square.

44. A quadrilateral with exactly one right angle.

The arrow indicates the right angle.

45. A rhombus.

Remember, every square is a rhombus.

46. A quadrilateral with exactly two right angles.

The arrows indicate the right angles.

47. A quadrilateral that has four acute angles.

48. A quadrilateral that can be cut into two acute triangles.

The dashed line divides the quadrilateral into two acute triangles.

Below, each description is connected to the correct shape for questions 43-48.

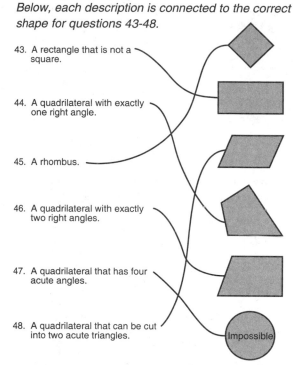

43. A rectangle that is not a square.

44. A quadrilateral with exactly one right angle.

45. A rhombus.

46. A quadrilateral with exactly two right angles.

47. A quadrilateral that has four acute angles.

48. A quadrilateral that can be cut into two acute triangles.

49. Since all squares have four sides and four right angles, all squares are rectangles. The statement is **true**.

50. Below is a rhombus that is not a square.

The statement is **false**.

51. Below is a quadrilateral that cannot be cut into two identical triangles.

The statement is **false**.

52. It is possible to connect any two identical triangles to make a quadrilateral. You can do this by attaching two sides that are the same length. For example, the pair of identical scalene obtuse triangles below can be connected to make six different quadrilaterals as shown:

The statement is **true**.

Notice that attaching two sides of identical right triangles does not *always* create a quadrilateral.

For example, you can attach two identical right triangles as shown to make a larger triangle. However, flipping one of the triangles or attaching the longest sides creates a quadrilateral.

53. Below is a quadrilateral that cannot be cut into two quadrilaterals by a straight line from the middle of one side to the middle of another side. The dashed lines show the six possible cuts from the middle of one side to the middle of another side.

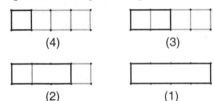

None of these six cuts splits the quadrilateral into two smaller quadrilaterals, so the statement is **false**.

54. There are a total of **3** rhombuses, as shown below:

55. There are 4 squares, 3 small rectangles, 2 medium rectangles, and 1 large rectangle.

(4)   (3)

(2)   (1)

There a total of 4+3+2+1 = **10** different rectangles.

56. There are 5 small squares, 4 medium squares, and 2 large squares.

(5)   (4)   (2)

There are a total of 5+4+2 = **11** different squares.

57. There are a total of **6** different rhombuses, as shown below.

58. There are a total of **15** rectangles!

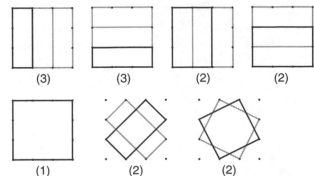
(3)   (3)   (2)   (2)

(1)   (2)   (2)

59. This shape has 10 sides, so it is a **decagon**.

60. This shape has 5 sides, so it is a **pentagon**.

61. This shape has 9 sides, so it is a **nonagon**.

62. This shape has 7 sides, so it is a **heptagon**.

63. This shape has 8 sides, so it is an **octagon**.

64. This shape has 6 sides, so it is a **hexagon**.

65. The two diagonals for each quadrilateral are drawn below:

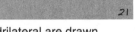

Notice that diagonals can be outside the boundary of a shape.

66. The diagonals of pentagon are drawn below.

Every pentagon has **5** diagonals.

67. The diagonals of a hexagon are drawn below.

Every hexagon has **9** diagonals.

68. The numbers of diagonals for a quadrilateral, pentagon, hexagon, heptagon, and octagon are 2, 5, 9, 14, and 20:

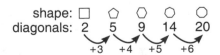
shape: □ ⬠ ⬡ ◯ ◯
diagonals: 2   5   9   14   20
                +3 +4 +5 +6

A pentagon has 3 more diagonals than a quadrilateral, a hexagon has 4 more diagonals than a pentagon, a heptagon has 5 more diagonals than a hexagon, and an octagon has 6 more diagonals than a heptagon. Based on the pattern, we guess that a nonagon will have 7 more diagonals than an octagon: 20+7 = **27** diagonals.

We can confirm this by drawing all 27 diagonals on a nonagon, as shown to the right.

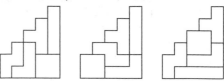

69. The five tetrominoes are often named for letters they resemble: I, L, O, S, and T, conveniently spelling "I LOST."

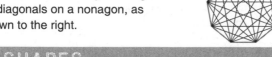

You may have drawn one or more of these tetrominoes flipped or turned in a different direction. Remember, if two polyominoes can be flipped or turned to look the same, they are considered the same polyomino.

70. Below are two possible solutions:

Every other solution can be flipped or turned to look the same as one of the two solutions above.

71. Below are two possible solutions:

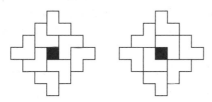

Every other solution can be flipped or turned to look the same as one of the two solutions above.

72. Below are four possible solutions:

Every other solution can be flipped to look the same as one of the solutions above.

73. Below are four possible solutions:

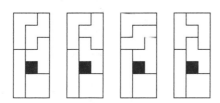

Every other solution can be flipped to look the same as one of the solutions above.

74. Below are three possible solutions:

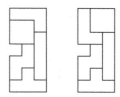

You may also have found one of the four other solutions.

75. Below are two possible solutions:

Every other solution can be flipped to look the same as one of the solutions above.

76. Below are three possible solutions:

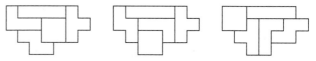

You may have found another solution.

77. Below are three possible solutions:

You may have found another solution.

78. If we color each octomino with light and dark squares like a chess board, the first and fourth octominoes each have a different number of light squares and dark squares:

Four dominoes will cover 4 dark and 4 light squares, so we cannot make the first and fourth shapes with dominoes. Next, we try to make the remaining three shapes with dominoes:

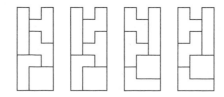

The second and third shapes can be made with dominoes as shown, but the fifth shape is impossible. Why? There is only one way to cover the bottom right square with a domino. Placing the domino as shown above makes it impossible to cover the lower left square. The three octominoes that are impossible are circled below:

79. If we color each large square with light and dark squares like a chess board, the first and third shapes each have 12 light squares and 12 dark squares. The second shape (in the middle) has 13 light squares and 11 dark squares.

Since 12 dominoes will always cover 12 light squares and 12 dark squares, **the middle shape** is impossible to make with dominoes.

Below are possible ways to make the other two shapes.

80. If we place a T-tetromino on a chess board, it will always cover either 3 light squares and 1 dark square, or 3 dark squares and 1 light square. A T-tetromino and four dominoes will cover either 5 light squares and 7 dark squares, or 7 light and 5 dark.

 or

If we color each shape with light and dark squares like a chess board, the 1st, 2nd, 4th, and 5th shapes each have 6 light squares and 6 dark squares. The third shape (in the middle) has 5 light squares and 7 dark squares. We could also color it with 7 light squares and 5 dark squares, but we cannot color it with the same number of light and dark squares.

So, **the middle shape** is the only one that can be tiled with one T-tetromino and four dominoes.

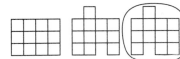

Four ways to make the shape are shown below.

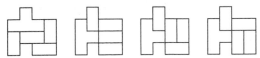

81. If we place the five tetrominoes on a chess board, each tetromino covers 2 light squares and 2 dark squares *except* the T-tetromino, which covers either 3 light squares and 1 dark square, or 3 dark squares and 1 light square.

   or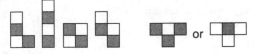

So, a set of five tetrominoes will cover either 9 light squares and 11 dark squares, or 11 light squares and 9 dark squares. If we color each shape with light and dark squares like a chess board, the first two shapes each have 9 light squares and 11 dark squares. The third shape (on the right) has 10 light squares and 10 dark squares.

Since the five tetrominoes will always cover a different number of light and dark squares, **the shape on the right** is impossible to make with the five tetrominoes.

Below is one way to make each of the first two shapes.

 SHAPES
Polyiamonds   32–33

82. The three tetriamonds are shown below.

You may have drawn one or more of these tetriamonds flipped or turned in a different direction. Remember, if two polyiamonds can be flipped or turned to look the same, they are the same polyiamond.

83. The four polyiamonds are shown below.

You may have drawn one or more of these pentiamonds flipped or turned in a different direction. Remember, if two polyiamonds can be flipped or turned to look the same, they are the same polyiamond.

84. Looking at the solution to Problem 82, we see that the first tetriamond is a triangle, the second is a quadrilateral, and the third is a hexagon. There is **1 triangle, 1 quadrilateral, 0 pentagons, and 1 hexagon**.

85. Looking at the solution to Problem 83, we see that the first pentiamond is a quadrilateral, the second is a pentagon, the third is a hexagon, and the fourth is a heptagon. There are **0 triangles, 1 quadrilateral, 1 pentagon, 1 hexagon, and 1 heptagon**.

86. Five toothpicks can make 2 triangles as shown below.

Other solutions may be flipped or turned to look like the one above.

87. Nine toothpicks can make 5 triangles as shown below. There are four small triangles and one large triangle.

Other solutions may be flipped or turned to look like the one above.

88. Nine toothpicks can make 3 rhombuses, as shown below.

You may also notice that the solution to the previous problem uses 9 toothpicks and creates 3 overlapping rhombuses! Other solutions may be flipped or turned to look like the ones above.

89. Six toothpicks can make 5 squares by crossing two toothpicks, as shown below. There are four small squares and one large square.

90. Two toothpicks can be moved as shown to make two triangles.

Other solutions may be flipped or turned to look like the one above.

91. Four toothpicks can be moved as shown to make two squares.

Other solutions may be flipped or turned to look like the one above.

92. For this problem, we first remove the three toothpicks shown in gray below:

This leaves three rhombuses. We can then use the three toothpicks we removed and one of the remaining sides to create a fourth rhombus. Two possible final arrangements are shown below.

93. Four toothpicks can be moved as shown to make three equilateral triangles. There are two small triangles and one large triangle.

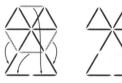

94. There are several ways to move four toothpicks to create three squares. Two of the ways are shown below.

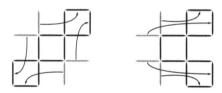

95. Two toothpicks can be moved as shown to leave four squares.

96. Removing the toothpicks shown in gray below leaves one small square and one large square.

97. There are 6 small triangles and 2 large triangles:

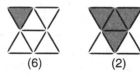

(6)   (2)

There are a total of 6+2 = **8** triangles.

98. Three toothpicks can be removed as shown to leave three equilateral triangles (one large and two small).

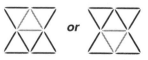

99. There are 9 small squares, 4 medium squares, and 1 large square:

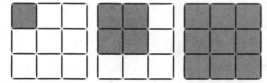

There are a total of $9+4+1 = $ **14** squares.

100. Four toothpicks can be removed to leave five squares as shown in the solutions below. In the first solution, there are five identical squares. In the next two solutions, there are four small squares and one large one.

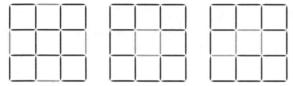

You may have found another way to leave four small squares and one large one by removing four toothpicks.

101. There are 9 small triangles, 3 medium triangles, and 1 large triangle:

There are a total of $9+3+1 = $ **13** equilateral triangles.

102. You must remove at least **6** toothpicks so that no triangles of any size are left. Three examples of how this can be done are shown below.

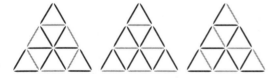

How do we know that it is not possible to eliminate every triangle by removing only 5 or fewer toothpicks? Look at the shaded triangles below:

None of these six shaded triangles overlap. So, we must remove at least one toothpick from each of the six shaded triangles above. Therefore, 6 is the smallest number of toothpicks that can be removed so that no triangles of any size are left.

SKIP-COUNTING
Basics
page 39

1. We begin at 2 and add 2's until we get to 20.

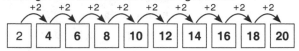

2. We begin at 5 and add 5's until we get to 50.

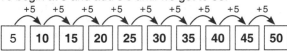

3. We begin at 3 and add 3's until we get to 30.

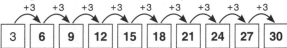

4. We begin at 10 and add 10's until we get to 100.

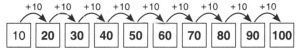

5. We begin at 11 and add 11's until we get to 110.

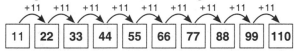

SKIP-COUNTING
Counting Objects
40-41

6. There are 11 pairs of choes. We can add eleven 2's by skip-counting.

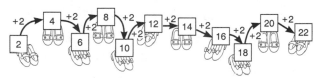

There are **22** shoes.

7. There are 9 tricycles, each with 3 wheels. We can add nine 3's by skip-counting.

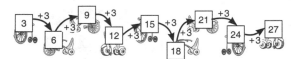

There are **27** wheels.

8. There are 5 groups, each with 5 pigeons. We can add five 5's by skip-counting.

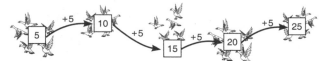

There are **25** pigeons.

9. There are 12 slumberbees, each with 6 legs. We can add twelve 6's by skip-counting.

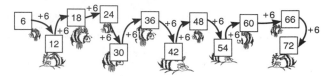

There are **72** legs on twelve slumberbees.

10. There are 8 octapugs, each with 8 legs. We can add eight 8's by skip-counting.

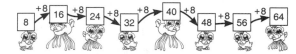

There are **64** legs on eight octapugs.

11. There are 11 flowers, each with 9 petals. We can add eleven 9's by sklp-counting.

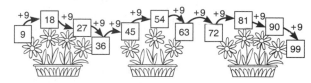

There are **99** flower petals.

12. There are 9 decagons, each with 10 sides. We can add nine 10's by skip-counting.

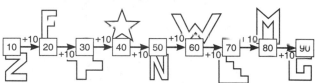

There are **90** sides on 9 decagons.

13. There are 9 porcupods, each with 15 spikes. We can add nine 15's by skip-counting.

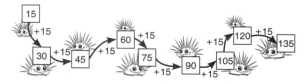

There are **135** spikes on 9 porcupods.

14. There are 8 spotted jackalopes, each with 50 spots. We can add eight 50's by skip-counting.

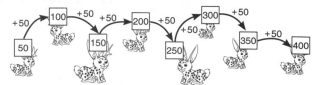

There are **400** spots on 8 spotted jackalopes.

15. There are 13 coins, each worth 25 cents. We can add thirteen 25's by skip-counting.

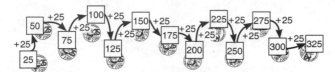

All together, the coins are worth **325** cents.

16. There are 6 gumballs in each group.

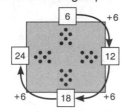

Grogg used **24** gumballs to make this pattern.

17. There are 3 gumballs in each group.

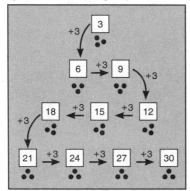

Grogg used **30** gumballs to make this pattern.

18. There are 12 gumballs in each group.

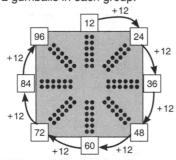

Grogg used **96** gumballs to make this pattern.

19. There are 4 rows of gumballs, each with 9 gumballs.

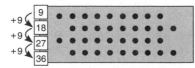

Grogg used **36** gumballs to make this pattern.

20. We see there is a square of 5 rows, each with 5 gumballs, plus one additional gumball.

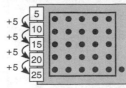

So, in the square there are 25 gumballs. Adding the extra gumball makes a total of 25+1 = 26 gumballs. Grogg used **26** gumballs to make this pattern.

21. If we tilt this pattern, we can count the gumballs in rows.

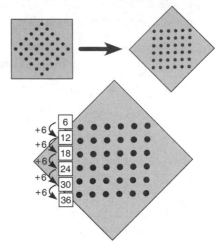

Grogg used **36** gumballs to make this pattern.

22. We can pretend that the two missing gumballs are there to make four rows of 8 gumballs.

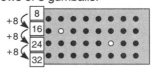

Then, we subtract the two missing gumballs:

32−2 = 30.
Grogg used **30** gumballs to make this pattern.

23. We can pretend that the five missing gumballs are there to make four rows of 10 gumballs.

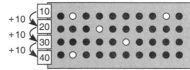

Then we subtract the five missing gumballs:

40−5 = 35.
Grogg used **35** gumballs in to make this pattern.

24. We can circle groups of 5 gumballs and skip-count.

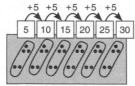

Grogg used **30** gumballs to make this pattern.

25. We can circle groups of 5 gumballs, then skip-count.

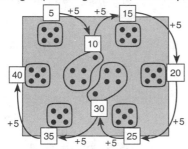

Grogg used **40** gumballs to make this pattern.

26. We can circle groups of 10 gumballs as shown and skip-count.

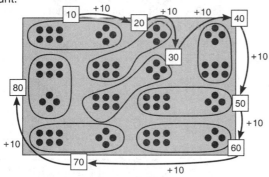

Grogg used **80** gumballs to make this pattern.

27. We can circle groups of 5 gumballs and skip-count.

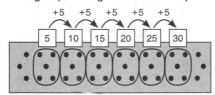

There are three extra gumballs on each side, so we add: 30+3+3 = 36. Grogg used **36** gumballs to make this pattern.

28. We can circle groups of 10 gumballs and skip-count.

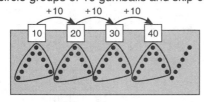

There are 6 extra gumballs, so we add six. 40+6 = 46. Grogg used **46** gumballs to make this pattern.

— or —

We can circle groups of 5 gumballs and skip-count.

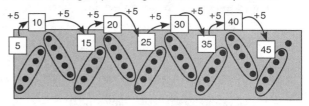

There is one extra gumball, so we add one. 45+1 = 46. Grogg used **46** gumballs to make this pattern.

SKIP-COUNTING
Hundred Charts 45-48

29. We mark all multiples of 2 with a ◱.

1	2	3	4	5	6	7	8	9	10
11	12	13	14	15	16	17	18	19	20
21	22	23	24	25	26	27	28	29	30
31	32	33	34	35	36	37	38	39	40
41	42	43	44	45	46	47	48	49	50
51	52	53	54	55	56	57	58	59	60
61	62	63	64	65	66	67	68	69	70
71	72	73	74	75	76	77	78	79	80
81	82	83	84	85	86	87	88	89	90
91	92	93	94	95	96	97	98	99	100

There are 5 columns marked, with 10 numbers in each column. We can skip-count to add five 10's.

10, 20, 30, 40, 50 (+10 each)

(You may have also noticed that exactly *half* of the 100 chart is marked with a ◱.)

There are **50** multiples of 2 in the 100 chart.

30. We mark all multiples of a 5 with a ◿.

1	2	3	4	5	6	7	8	9	10
11	12	13	14	15	16	17	18	19	20
21	22	23	24	25	26	27	28	29	30
31	32	33	34	35	36	37	38	39	40
41	42	43	44	45	46	47	48	49	50
51	52	53	54	55	56	57	58	59	60
61	62	63	64	65	66	67	68	69	70
71	72	73	74	75	76	77	78	79	80
81	82	83	84	85	86	87	88	89	90
91	92	93	94	95	96	97	98	99	100

We have marked two columns of 10 numbers with a ◿.

So, there are 10+10 = **20** multiples of 5 on the 100 chart.

31. The following ten numbers are marked with a ⊠:

10, 20, 30, 40, 50, 60, 70, 80, 90, 100.

32. The ten numbers in the 100 chart that are multiples of both 2 and 5 are 10, 20, 30, 40, 50, 60, 70, 80, 90, and 100. These are the numbers that we use to skip-count by 10's.

$$\overset{+10}{\frown}\ \overset{+10}{\frown}\ \overset{+10}{\frown}\ \overset{+10}{\frown}\ \overset{+10}{\frown}\ \overset{+10}{\frown}\ \overset{+10}{\frown}\ \overset{+10}{\frown}\ \overset{+10}{\frown}$$
10, 20, 30, 40, 50, 60, 70, 80, 90, $\boxed{100}$

These numbers are all multiples of 10.
If a number is a multiple of both 2 and 5, it is also a multiple of **10**.

33. In the marked hundred chart (see Problem 30), there are four columns of 10 numbers each that are not marked with a 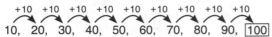. We can skip-count to add four 10's.

$$\overset{+10}{\frown}\ \overset{+10}{\frown}\ \overset{+10}{\frown}$$
10, 20, 30, 40

There are **40** numbers in the 100 chart that are not a multiple of 2 or a multiple of 5.

34. We mark all multiples of 8 with a ◪.

1	2	3	4	5	6	7	8	9	10
11	12	13	14	15	16	17	18	19	20
21	22	23	24	25	26	27	28	29	30
31	32	33	34	35	36	37	38	39	40
41	42	43	44	45	46	47	48	49	50
51	52	53	54	55	56	57	58	59	60
61	62	63	64	65	66	67	68	69	70
71	72	73	74	75	76	77	78	79	80
81	82	83	84	85	86	87	88	89	90
91	92	93	94	95	96	97	98	99	100

There are **12** multiples of 8 in the 100 chart.

35. We mark all multiples of a 3 with a ◩.

1	2	3	4	5	6	7	8	9	10
11	12	13	14	15	16	17	18	19	20
21	22	23	24	25	26	27	28	29	30
31	32	33	34	35	36	37	38	39	40
41	42	43	44	45	46	47	48	49	50
51	52	53	54	55	56	57	58	59	60
61	62	63	64	65	66	67	68	69	70
71	72	73	74	75	76	77	78	79	80
81	82	83	84	85	86	87	88	89	90
91	92	93	94	95	96	97	98	99	100

We count **33** multiples of 3 on the 100 chart.

36. The following four numbers are marked with a ⊠:
24, 48, 72, 96.

37. The four numbers in the 100 chart that are multiples of both 8 and 3 are 24, 48, 72, and 96. We look for a pattern: $24+24=48.$ $48+24=72.$ $72+24=96.$

We are adding 24 over and over.

$$\overset{+24}{\frown}\ \overset{+24}{\frown}\ \overset{+24}{\frown}$$
24, 48, 72, 96...

24 is the smallest multiple of both 8 and 3. So, to find the next multiple of both 8 and 3, we continue the pattern: $96+24=120.$

$$\overset{+24}{\frown}\ \overset{+24}{\frown}\ \overset{+24}{\frown}\ \overset{+24}{\frown}$$
24, 48, 72, 96, $\boxed{120}$

The smallest number over 100 that is a multiple of both 8 and 3 is **120**.

38. The five numbers we found that are multiples of both 8 and 3 are 24, 48, 72, 96, and 120. These are the numbers that we use to skip-count by 24's.

$$\overset{+24}{\frown}\ \overset{+24}{\frown}\ \overset{+24}{\frown}\ \overset{+24}{\frown}$$
24, 48, 72, 96, 120

So, these numbers are all multiples of 24. If a number is a multiple of both 8 and 3, it is a multiple of **24**.

39. We mark all multiples of 4 with a ◪.

1	2	3	4	5	6	7	8	9	10
11	12	13	14	15	16	17	18	19	20
21	22	23	24	25	26	27	28	29	30
31	32	33	34	35	36	37	38	39	40
41	42	43	44	45	46	47	48	49	50
51	52	53	54	55	56	57	58	59	60
61	62	63	64	65	66	67	68	69	70
71	72	73	74	75	76	77	78	79	80
81	82	83	84	85	86	87	88	89	90
91	92	93	94	95	96	97	98	99	100

There are 5 numbers in each of 5 columns marked with a ◪. We can skip-count to add five 5's.

$$\overset{+5}{\frown}\ \overset{+5}{\frown}\ \overset{+5}{\frown}\ \overset{+5}{\frown}$$
5, 10, 15, 20, 25

So, there are **25** multiples of 4 in the 100 chart.

40. We mark all multiples of a 6 with a ◩.

1	2	3	4	5	6	7	8	9	10
11	12	13	14	15	16	17	18	19	20
21	22	23	24	25	26	27	28	29	30
31	32	33	34	35	36	37	38	39	40
41	42	43	44	45	46	47	48	49	50
51	52	53	54	55	56	57	58	59	60
61	62	63	64	65	66	67	68	69	70
71	72	73	74	75	76	77	78	79	80
81	82	83	84	85	86	87	88	89	90
91	92	93	94	95	96	97	98	99	100

There are **16** multiples of 6 in the 100 chart.

41. The following numbers are marked with a ⊠:

12, 24, 36, 48, 60, 72, 84, 96.

8 numbers in the chart are multiples of both 4 and 6.

42. The numbers in our 100 chart that are multiples of both 4 and 6 are 12, 24, 36, 48, 60, 72, 84, 96. We look for a pattern: 12+12 = 24. 24+12 = 36. 36+12 = 48.
48+12 = 60. 60+12 = 72. 72+12 = 84.
84+12 = 96.

We are adding 12 over and over. These are the numbers that we use to skip-count by 12's.

$$\overset{+12}{\frown}\ \overset{+12}{\frown}\ \overset{+12}{\frown}\ \overset{+12}{\frown}\ \overset{+12}{\frown}\ \overset{+12}{\frown}\ \overset{+12}{\frown}$$
12, 24, 36, 48, 60, 72, 84, 96

These numbers are all multiples of 12. If a number is a multiple of both 4 and 6, it is a multiple of **12**.

43. Multiples of 4 are marked with a ◺. Multiples of 6 are marked with a ◹. We can shade multiples of 5.

1	2	3	4	5	6	7	8	9	10
11	12	13	14	15	16	17	18	19	20
21	22	23	24	25	26	27	28	29	30
31	32	33	34	35	36	37	38	39	40
41	42	43	44	45	46	47	48	49	50
51	52	53	54	55	56	57	58	59	60
61	62	63	64	65	66	67	68	69	70
71	72	73	74	75	76	77	78	79	80
81	82	83	84	85	86	87	88	89	90
91	92	93	94	95	96	97	98	99	100

Any number that is shaded *and* marked with a ⊠ is a multiple of 4, 5, and 6. The only number in the 100 chart that is both shaded and marked with a ⊠ is **60**.

44. In Problem 31, we list all ten multiples of 10 in the 100 chart. So, Cammie's number must be **10**.

How do we know there isn't another number with 10 multiples in the hundreds chart?

We look at the numbers one more and one less than 10. There are only nine multiples of 11 in the 100 chart (11, 22, 33, 44, 55, 66, 77, 88, and 99), and every number greater than 11 has fewer than ten multiples in the 100 chart.

There are eleven multiples of 9 in the 100 chart (9, 18, 27, 36, 45, 54, 63, 72, 81, 90, 99). Every number less than 9 has more than ten multiples in the 100 chart.

45. In Problem 35, we see that there are exactly 33 multiples of 3 in the 100 chart. Those multiples include the numbers 18, 33, and 90. So, Lizzie's number must be **3**.

There are 25 multiples of 4 in the 100 chart, and every number greater than 4 has fewer multiples in the 100 chart. There are 50 multiples of 2 in the 100 chart, and 100 multiples of 1 in the 100 chart. So, 3 is the only number with 33 multiples in the 100 chart.

46. In Problems 30, 39 and 40, we see that each of 4, 5 and 6 has exactly two multiples in the 30's. Since 42 is a multiple of 6, but not of 4 or 5, Ralph's number is **6**.

47. In Problem 30, we see that 5 has exactly two multiples in the 20's (20 and 25), exactly two multiples in the 30's (30 and 35), and exactly two multiples in the 40's (40 and 45). No other number has exactly two multiples in each of the 20's, 30's and 40's, so Alex's number must be **5**.

48. In Problem 41, we see that there are exactly 8 numbers in the 100 chart that are multiples of both 4 and 6. In Problem 42, we found that all numbers that are multiples of 4 and 6 are multiples of 12. So, there are exactly 8 multiples of 12 in the 100 chart. Winnie's number is **12**.

There are 7 multiples of 13 in the 100 chart (13, 26, 39, 52, 65, 78, and 91), and every number greater than 13 has fewer multiples in the 100 chart. There are nine multiples of 11 in the 100 chart (11, 22, 33, 44, 55, 66, 77, 88, and 99), and every number smaller than 11 has more multiples in the 100 chart. So, 12 is the only number with 8 multiples in the 100 chart.

SKIP-COUNTING
Finding Patterns 49-50

49. We skip-count by 2's, beginning at 1.

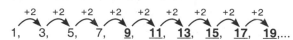
1, 3, 5, 7, **9**, **11**, **13**, **15**, **17**, **19**,...

50. We skip-count by 8's, beginning at 9.

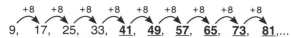
9, 17, 25, 33, **41**, **49**, **57**, **65**, **73**, **81**,...

51. We skip-count by 3's, beginning at 4.

4, 7, 10, 13, **16**, **19**, **22**, **25**, **28**, **31**,...

52. We skip-count by 4's, beginning at 3.

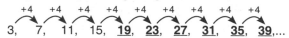
3, 7, 11, 15, **19**, **23**, **27**, **31**, **35**, **39**,...

53. We skip-count by 9's, beginning at 5.

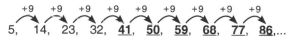
5, 14, 23, 32, **41**, **50**, **59**, **68**, **77**, **86**,...

54. We skip-count by 7's, beginning at 29.

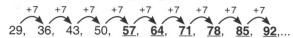
29, 36, 43, 50, **57**, **64**, **71**, **78**, **85**, **92**,...

55. We skip-count by 5's, beginning at 98.

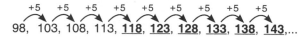
98, 103, 108, 113, **118**, **123**, **128**, **133**, **138**, **143**,...

56. 4+4 = 8 and 28+4 = 32.
So, we skip-count by 4's, beginning at 4.

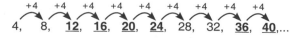
4, 8, **12**, **16**, **20**, **24**, 28, 32, **36**, **40**,...

57. $35 + 5 = 40$. So, we skip-count by 5's, beginning at 5.

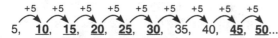

5, __**10**__, __**15**__, __**20**__, __**25**__, __**30**__, 35, 40, __**45**__, __**50**__...

58. $12 + 6 = 18$. So, we skip-count by 6's.

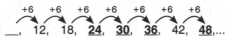

__, 12, 18, __**24**__, __**30**__, __**36**__, 42, __**48**__,...

We work backwards to find the first number in the pattern: ☐ $+ 6 = 12$. Since $12 - 6 = 6$, we get $\boxed{6} + 6 = 12$. The first number in the pattern is 6.

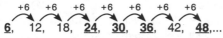

__**6**__, 12, 18, __**24**__, __**30**__, __**36**__, 42, __**48**__,...

59. $81 + 2 = 83$. So, we skip-count by 2's, beginning at 73.

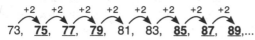

73, __**75**__, __**77**__, __**79**__, 81, 83, __**85**__, __**87**__, __**89**__,...

60. $5 + 4 = 9$. So, we skip-count by 4's, beginning at 5.

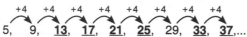

5, 9, __**13**__, __**17**__, __**21**__, __**25**__, 29, __**33**__, __**37**__,...

61. We look at the two closest numbers given in our pattern, 49 and 63.

49, __, 63,...

We look for the number that we can add to 49 twice to get 63. Because $63 - 49 = 14$, to get from 49 to 63, we need to add 14. Since $7 + 7 = 14$, we can add 7 twice to get 14. So, we are skip-counting by 7's.

49, __**56**__, 63,...

You may have also noticed that 21, 49, and 63 are all multiples of 7. We skip-count by 7's to fill in more missing numbers.

__, __, 21, __**28**__, __**35**__, __**42**__, 49, __**56**__, 63,...

When skip-counting by 7's, we add 7 to get the next number. To get the previous term, we can do the opposite: subtract 7. We work backwards from 21 by subtracting to find the first two numbers in the pattern.

__**7**__, __**14**__, 21, __**28**__, __**35**__, __**42**__, 49, __**56**__, 63,...

62. We look at the two closest numbers given in our pattern, 56 and 72.

56, __, 72,...

We look for the number that we can add to 56 twice to get 72. Subtracting, we get $72 - 56 = 16$. Since $8 + 8 = 16$, we can add 8 twice to get 16. So, we are skip-counting by 8's.

56, __**64**__, 72,...

We skip-count by 8's to fill in more missing numbers.

__, __, __, 32, __**40**__, __**48**__, 56, __**64**__, 72,...

We work backwards to find the first three numbers in the pattern.

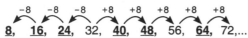

__**8**__, __**16**__, __**24**__, 32, __**40**__, __**48**__, 56, __**64**__, 72,...

63. We look at the two closest numbers given in our pattern, 26 and 38.

26, __, __, 38...

We look for a number that we can add to 26 three times to get 38. Subtracting, we get $38 - 26 = 12$. Since $4 + 4 + 4 = 12$, we can add 4 three times to get 12. So, we are skip-counting by 4's.

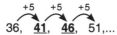

26, __**30**__, __**34**__, 38,...

We can skip-count by 4's to fill in more missing numbers.

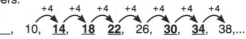

__, 10, __**14**__, __**18**__, __**22**__, 26, __**30**__, __**34**__, 38,...

We work backwards to find the first number in the pattern.

__**6**__, 10, __**14**__, __**18**__, __**22**__, 26, __**30**__, __**34**__, 38,...

64. We look at the two closest numbers given in our pattern, 36 and 51.

36, __, __, 51,...

We look for a number that we can add to 36 three times to get 51. Subtracting, we get $51 - 36 = 15$. Since $5 + 5 + 5 = 15$, we can add 5 three times to get 15. So, we are skip-counting by 5's.

36, __**41**__, __**46**__, 51,...

We can skip-count by 5's to fill in more missing numbers.

__, __, 36, __**41**__, __**46**__, 51, __**56**__, __**61**__, __**66**__, 71,...

We work backwards to find the first two numbers in the pattern.

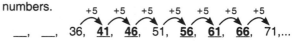

__**26**__, __**31**__, 36, __**41**__, __**46**__, 51, __**56**__, __**61**__, __**66**__, 71,...

65. We skip-count by 5's, beginning at 3.

20	30	21	3	18
16	23	28	33	38
13	18	11	15	17
8	3	6	14	16
7	4	9	12	14

66. We skip-count by 11's, beginning at 13.

35	37	45	53	61
21	13	24	35	69
5	16	56	46	77
21	79	68	57	85
101	90	43	62	90

67. We skip-count by 4's, beginning at 2.

24	20	25	5	18
23	16	9	2	10
42	38	11	6	26
52	34	16	10	14
15	30	26	22	18

68. We skip-count by 3's, beginning at 6.

10	12	14	15	18
8	6	9	12	21
4	7	14	25	24
2	8	17	30	27
12	9	15	33	32

69. We skip-count by 8's, beginning at 4.

52	91	13	22	31
52	15	4	28	36
63	26	12	20	44
84	76	68	60	52
25	17	82	25	16

70. We skip-count by 9's, beginning at 5.

90	5	86	50	31
104	95	42	73	27
92	86	13	17	21
68	77	9	5	14
59	50	41	32	23

71. We skip-count by 4's, beginning at 17.

52	37	47	28	64
22	27	57	53	57
21	17	20	49	71
25	53	14	45	52
29	33	37	41	47

72. We skip count by 7's, beginning at 9.

22	15	21	27	33
16	9	13	76	18
23	18	15	23	43
30	37	44	33	50
14	26	51	58	35

73. We skip-count by 4's, beginning at 20.

15	90	15	27	34	41
70	80	30	20	24	48
60	50	40	22	28	32
65	60	56	52	39	36
31	64	68	48	44	40
51	76	72	85	56	42

74. We skip-count by 12's, beginning at 23.

127	135	143	151	159	175
119	59	71	83	167	179
111	47	36	95	155	143
103	35	23	107	119	131
95	82	31	39	47	142
87	79	71	63	55	73

SKIP-COUNTING
Word Problems
53-58

75. There were 5 students at each of 4 tables. We can add four 5's by skip-counting:

5, 10, 15, 20.

There were **20** students in class that day.

76. Lizzie reads 12 pages each night for 9 nights. We can add nine 12's by skip-counting:

12, 24, 36, 48, 60, 72, 84, 96, 108.

Lizzie reads **108** pages in 9 days.

77. A triangle has 3 sides, so we can add this number 111 times. Adding 111 threes is the same as adding three 111's.

$$111+111+111=333.$$

All together, 111 triangles have **333** sides.

78. We write out the list of numbers that Grogg said:

100, 200, 300, 400, 500, 600, 700, 800, 900, 1000, 1100, 1200, 1300, 1400, 1500, 1600, 1700, ...

The 17th number Grogg says is **1,700**.

— *or* —

When we skip-count, we add the same number over and over again. The first number Grogg says is 100. So, to find the 17th number Grogg says, we add seventeen 100's to get **1,700**.

79. Adding 12 a thousand times is the same as adding 1,000 twelve times. Twelve thousands is 12,000. So, the 1,000th number that Alex says is **12,000**.

80. Adding twenty 6's is the same as adding six 20's. We can add six 20's by skip-counting:

20, 40, 60, 80, 100, 120.

The 20th number Lizzie says is **120**.

81. In the pattern, we begin at 7 and skip-count by 7's. To find the 50th number in the pattern, we add fifty 7's. Adding fifty 7's is the same as adding seven 50's, and we can add seven 50's by skip-counting.

$$50, 100, 150, 200, 250, 300, \boxed{350}.$$

The 50th number in the pattern is **350**.

82. The difference of 70 and 54 is 16. So, we can add 16 to get from 54 to 70. Winnie never says 70, so she cannot be skip-counting by 16's. Since $8+8=16$, adding two 8's is the same as adding 16. So, Winnie cannot be skip-counting by 8's. Adding four 4's or eight 2's also gives us 16, so she cannot be skip-counting by 4's or 2's.

$$\cancel{2} \quad \cancel{4} \quad 6 \quad \cancel{8} \quad \cancel{16}$$

If Winnie begins at 54 and skip-counts by 6's, she can skip-count higher than 70 without saying 70:

$$54, 60, 66, 72, ...$$

So, Winnie could only have skip-counted by **6**'s.

83. The difference of 35 and 5 is 30. So, we can add 30 to get from 5 to 35. Ralph never says 35, so he cannot be skip-counting by 30's. Since $5+5+5+5+5+5=30$, adding six 5's is the same as adding 30. So, Ralph cannot be skip-counting by 5's. Adding ten 3's or fifteen 2's also gives us 30, so he cannot be skip-counting by 3's or 2's.

$$\cancel{2} \quad \cancel{3} \quad 4 \quad \cancel{5} \quad \cancel{30}$$

If Ralph begins at 5 and skip-counts by 4's, he can skip-count higher than 35 without saying 35:

$$5, 9, 13, 17, 21, 25, 29, 33, 37, ...$$

So, Ralph could only have skip-counted by **4**'s.

84. The difference of 68 and 23 is 45. So, we can add 45 to get from 23 to 68. Since $15+15+15=45$, adding three 15's or fifteen 3's is the same as adding 45. So, Cammie could be skip-counting by 15's or 3's. Since $9+9+9+9+9=45$, adding five 9's or nine 5's is the same as adding 45. So, she could also be skip-counting by 9's or 5's. If Cammie begins at an odd number (like 23) and skip-counts by 2's, she will only say odd numbers:

$$23, 25, 27, 29, 31, 33, 35, ...$$

68 is not odd. So, Cammie cannot begin at 23 and skip-count by **2**'s to 68.

85. The difference of 65 and 9 is 56. So, we can add 56 to get from 9 to 65. Adding seven 8's or eight 7's is the same as adding 56. So, Grogg could be skip-counting by 8's or 7's. Adding two 4's or four 2's is the same as adding 8. So, adding fourteen 4's or twenty-eight 2's is the same as adding seven 8's. So, he could also be skip-counting by 4's or 2's. If Grogg begins at 9 and skip-counts by 9's, he will not say 65:

$$9, 18, 27, 36, 45, 54, 63, 72, ...$$

So, Grogg cannot begin at 9 and skip-count by **9**'s to 65.

86. We list some numbers that Lizzie and Winnie say:

Lizzie: 10, 20, **30**, 40, 50, 60, 70, 80, ...
Winnie: 6, 12, 18, 24, **30**, 36, 42, ...

The smallest number Lizzie and Winnie both say is **30**.

87. We list some numbers that Winnie and Grogg say:

Winnie: 9, 18, 27, **36**, 45, 54, 63, ...
Grogg: 4, 8, 12, 16, 20, 24, 28, 32, **36**, ...

The smallest number Winnie and Grogg both say is **36**.

88. We list some numbers that Grogg and Alex say:

Grogg: 2, 10, 18, **26**, 34, 42, 50, ...
Alex: 2, 5, 8, 11, 14, 17, 20, 23, **26**, 29, ...

The smallest number after 2 that Grogg and Alex both say is **26**.

89. We list some numbers that Alex and Lizzie say:

Alex: 4, 11, 18, 25, 32, 39, **46**, 53, ...
Lizzie: 4, 10, 16, 22, 28, 34, 40, **46**, ...

The smallest number after 4 that Alex and Lizzie both say is **46**.

90. We list some numbers that Winnie and Alex say:

Winnie: 6, 9, 12, 15, 18, 21, 24, **27**, 30,...
Alex: 3, 11, 19, **27**, 35, 41, ...

The smallest number Winnie and Alex both say is **27**.

91. Cammie skip-counts by 5's and says "5, 10, 15, 20, ..." The first number Lizzie and Cammie both say is 15, so Lizzie must be skip-counting by a *different* number than Cammie. Cammie adds three 5's to get to 15. Adding three 5's is the same as adding five 3's, so we guess that Lizzie could be skip-counting by 3's, beginning at 0:

$$0, 3, 6, 9, 12, \underline{15}, 18, 21, ...$$

If Lizzie begins at 0 and skip-counts by 2's, 4's, 6's, 7's, 8's, or 9's, then she will never say 15. So, Lizzie must be skip-counting by **3**'s.

92. Since there is one extra member when the choir stands in rows of 8, the number of students in the choir is one more than a multiple of 8. So, we can begin at 1 and skip-count by 8's:

$$1, 9, 17, 25, 33, 41, 49, 57, 65, ...$$

57 is the only number that is 1 more than a multiple of 8 *and* between 50 and 60. So, there are **57** students in the Beast Academy choir.

93. If seated in rows of 7, there will be one extra monster. So, the number of monsters who will attend the talent show is one more than a multiple of 7. We can begin at 1 and skip-count by 7's to create a list for the possible numbers of monsters who will attend the talent show:

$$1, 8, 15, 22, 29, 36, 43, 50, 57, 64, 71, 78, 85, 92, 99, ...$$

Since there will be no monsters left over if they sit in rows of 11, the number of monsters who will attend the talent show is a multiple of 11. We compare our list above to the multiples of 11:

$$11, 22, 33, 44, 55, 66, 77, 88, 99, ...$$

The only number between 70 and 100 on both lists is 99. So, **99** monsters will attend the Beast Academy Talent Show.

94. We are skip-counting by 6's, starting at 8.
We can continue the pattern to find the 11th number:

$$\overset{+6}{\frown}\ \overset{+6}{\frown}\ \overset{+6}{\frown}\ \overset{+6}{\frown}\ \overset{+6}{\frown}\ \overset{+6}{\frown}\ \overset{+6}{\frown}\ \overset{+6}{\frown}\ \overset{+6}{\frown}\ \overset{+6}{\frown}$$
8, 14, 20, 26, 32, 38, 44, 50, 56, 62, $\boxed{68}$

The 11th number in the pattern is **68**.

Notice that we started at 8 and added ten 6's to get the 11th number of the pattern. Adding ten 6's is the same as adding six 10's. So, we could have also found the 11th number by starting at 8 and adding six 10's:

$$\overset{+10}{\frown}\ \overset{+10}{\frown}\ \overset{+10}{\frown}\ \overset{+10}{\frown}\ \overset{+10}{\frown}\ \overset{+10}{\frown}$$
8, 18, 28, 38, 48, 58, $\boxed{68}$

95. We are skip-counting by 9's, starting at 5.
To find the 101st number in the pattern, we start at 5 and then add one hundred 9's. Adding one hundred 9's is the same as adding nine 100's. So, we can also find the 101st number by starting at 5 and adding nine 100's. Nine 100's is 900, so the 101st number is $5+900=$ **905**.

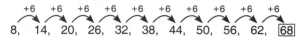

SKIP-COUNTING
Balancing Weights   59-63

96. To count the number of grams in fifteen 7-gram weights, we can skip-count to add fifteen 7's or seven 15's:

15, 30, 45, 60, 75, 90, $\boxed{105}$.

The elefinch's weight is **105 grams**.

97. We can skip-count by 5's to 60:

5, 10, 15, 20, 25, 30, 35, 40, 45, 50, 55, $\boxed{60}$.

This is twelve 5's. So, Grogg balanced a 60-gram pandakeet with **12** five-gram weights.

98. We can skip-count by 5's to 85:

5, 10, 15, 20, 25, 30, 35, 40, 45,
50, 55, 60, 65, 70, 75, 80, 85.

This is seventeen 5's. So, Ralph balanced an 85-gram pandakeet with **17** five-gram weights.

— *or* —

We could have also used our work from Problem 97: Grogg used twelve 5-gram weights to balance 60 grams. Skip-counting from 60 to 85 will tell us how many *more* weights Ralph will need:

$$\overset{+5}{\frown}\ \overset{+5}{\frown}\ \overset{+5}{\frown}\ \overset{+5}{\frown}\ \overset{+5}{\frown}$$
60, 65, 70, 75, 80, 85

Ralph needs five *more* weights than Grogg needed. So, all together, he needs $12+5=$ **17** five-gram weights to balance an 85-gram pandakeet.

99. We can skip-count by 3's to 27:

3, 6, 9, 12, 15, 18, 21, 24, 27.

This is nine 3's. So, Lizzie balances a 27-gram octapug with **9** three-gram weights.

100. The difference of 66 and 45 is 21. So, the 66-gram octapug weighs 21 grams more than the 45-gram octapug. We can skip-count by 3's to 21 to find how many more weights are required to balance the heavier octapug:

3, 6, 9, 12, 15, 18, 21.

That is seven 3's. Lizzie will need **7** more 3-gram weights.

— *or* —

If we skip-count by 3's from 45 to 66, we will find out how many more weights Lizzie will need.

$$\overset{+3}{\frown}\ \overset{+3}{\frown}\ \overset{+3}{\frown}\ \overset{+3}{\frown}\ \overset{+3}{\frown}\ \overset{+3}{\frown}\ \overset{+3}{\frown}$$
45, 48, 51, 54, 57, 60, 63, $\boxed{66}$

We added seven more 3's to get from 45 to 66, so Lizzie will need **7** more 3-gram weights.

101. If we skip-count by 3's, we will say 15:

3, 6, 9, 12, 15, ...

Adding five 3's gives us 15, so **yes, we can balance 15 grams using five 3-gram weights.**

102. If we skip-count by 4's, we will never say 27:

4, 8, 12, 16, 20, 24, 28, 32, ...

No, we cannot balance 27 grams with only 4-gram weights.

103. $5+5+8=18$. So, we can balance 18 grams using two 5-gram weights and one 8-gram weight. All together, we use $2+1=$ **3** weights.

104. $7+7+7+7+11=39$. So, we can balance 39 grams using four 7-gram weights and one 11-gram weight. All together, we use $4+1=$ **5** weights.

105. We could add ten 4-gram weights to balance 40 grams: $4+4+4+4+4+4+4+4+4+4=40$.
Nine 4-gram weights balance the same weight as four 9-gram weights, so we can trade nine 4-gram weights for four 9-gram weights. Then, we can balance 40 grams using one 4-gram weight and four 9-gram weights: $4+9+9+9+9=40$. The smallest number of weights we could use is $1+4=$ **5**. Notice that we use fewer weights when we use more of the larger weights.

106. We could balance 44 grams with ten 3-gram weights and two 7-gram weights.
$3+3+3+3+3+3+3+3+3+3+7+7=44$.
Seven 3-gram weights balance the same weight as three 7-gram weights. So, we can trade seven 3-gram weights for three 7-gram weights. Then, we can balance 44 grams with three 3-gram weights and five 7-gram weights: $3+3+3+7+7+7+7+7=44$. The smallest number of weights we could use is $3+5=$ **8**.

107. We shade all the weights that can be balanced using 2-gram and 13-gram weights.

Since we can balance 2 grams with one 2-gram weight, we shade 2. We can balance 4 grams with two 2-gram weights, so we shade 4. Similarly, we can continue to shade all of the multiples of 2.

We also shade 13 because we can balance 13 grams with one 13-gram weight.

1	2	3	4	5	6	7	8	9	10	11	12	13
14	15	16	17	18	19	20	21	22	23	24	25	26
27	28	29	30	31	32	33	34	35	36	37	38	39
40	41	42	43	44	45	46	47	48	49	50	51	52

Any number *below* a shaded number can also be shaded. Since our chart has rows of 13, moving down one row is the same as adding 13. For example, since we can balance 2 grams, we can also balance all of the numbers below 2 on the chart by adding 13-gram weights.

1	2	3	4	5	6	7	8	9	10	11	12	13
14	15	16	17	18	19	20	21	22	23	24	25	26
27	28	29	30	31	32	33	34	35	36	37	38	39
40	41	42	43	44	45	46	47	48	49	50	51	52

The shaded squares are all the weights that can be balanced. All the weights from the second row down can be balanced.

We cannot balance 1, 3, 5, 7, 9, or 11 grams. So, there are **6** different weights that cannot be balanced.

108. We shade all the weights that can be balanced using 3-gram and 7-gram weights.

1	2	3	4	5	6	7
8	9	10	11	12	13	14
15	16	17	18	19	20	21
22	23	24	25	26	27	28
29	30	31	32	33	34	35

The largest number of grams we cannot balance using 3-gram and 7-gram weights is **11** grams.

109. We set up a chart as in the previous problems, shading all the weights that *can* be balanced using 5-gram and 7-gram weights. The charts can be most helpful if drawn with rows of 5 or 7, since these are the weights used in the problem.

1	2	3	4	5	6	7
8	9	10	11	12	13	14
15	16	17	18	19	20	21
22	23	24	25	26	27	28
29	30	31	32	33	34	35
36	37	38	39	40	41	42

1	2	3	4	5
6	7	8	9	10
11	12	13	14	15
16	17	18	19	20
21	22	23	24	25
26	27	28	29	30
31	32	33	34	35

Now, we see the largest number of grams we cannot balance using 5-gram and 7-gram weights is **23** grams.

110. We set up a chart as in the previous problems, shading all the weights that *can* be balanced using 4-gram and 9-gram weights.

1	2	3	4	5	6	7	8	9
10	11	12	13	14	15	16	17	18
19	20	21	22	23	24	25	26	27
28	29	30	31	32	33	34	35	36
37	38	39	40	41	42	43	44	45

1	2	3	4
5	6	7	8
9	10	11	12
13	14	15	16
17	18	19	20
21	22	23	24
25	26	27	28
39	30	31	32

In both charts, we see that the largest number of grams we cannot balance using 4-gram and 9-gram weights is **23** grams.

111. We set up a chart as in the previous problems, shading all the weights that *can* be balanced using 3-gram and 8-gram weights.

1	2	3	4	5	6	7	8
9	10	11	12	13	14	15	16
17	18	19	20	21	22	23	24
25	26	27	28	29	30	31	32
33	34	35	36	37	38	39	40
41	42	43	44	45	46	47	48

1	2	3
4	5	6
7	8	9
10	11	12
13	14	15
16	17	18
19	20	21

In both charts, we see that the largest number of grams we cannot balance using 3-gram and 8-gram weights is **13** grams.

112. We set up a chart as in the previous problems, shading all the weights that *can* be balanced using 4-gram and 6-gram weights.

1	2	3	4	5	6
7	8	9	10	11	12
13	14	15	16	17	18
19	20	21	22	23	24
25	26	27	28	29	30
31	32	33	34	35	36
37	38	39	40	41	42

1	2	3	4
5	6	7	8
9	10	11	12
13	14	15	16
17	18	19	20
21	22	23	24
25	26	27	28
39	30	31	32

In both charts, we see that **we will never be able to balance any odd number of grams using only 4-gram and 6-gram weights. So, there is no largest number of grams that we cannot balance.**

PERIMETER & AREA — *Basics* — Page 65

1. $(9+11)+12 = 20+12 = \mathbf{32}$.

2. $(15+5)+(7+13) = 20+20 = \mathbf{40}$.

3. $(8+12)+14 = 20+14 = \mathbf{34}$.

4. $(8+12)+(14+6) = 20+20 = \mathbf{40}$.

PERIMETER & AREA — *Regular Polygons* — 66

5. Every side of the regular pentagon is the same length.

6. Perimeter $= 4+4+4+4+4 = \mathbf{20}$.

7. Perimeter $= 6+6+6+6 = \mathbf{24}$.

8. Perimeter $= 3+3+3+3+3+3+3+3+3 = \mathbf{27}$.

9. Perimeter $= 7+7+7+7+7 = \mathbf{35}$.

10. Because $10+10+10+10+10+10 = 60$, each side has length **10**.

PERIMETER & AREA — *Rectangles* — 67

11. Opposite sides of a rectangle are the same length.

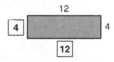

12. Perimeter $= (12+4)+(12+4) = 16+16 = \mathbf{32}$.

13. $(13+7)+(13+7) = 20+20 = \mathbf{40}$.

14. $(8+16)+(8+16) = 24+24 = \mathbf{48}$.

15. To find the perimeter of a rectangle, we can add its height and width, then double the result. When we double a whole number, the result is always even. Because 13 is odd, **it is impossible to draw a rectangle with whole number side lengths and perimeter 13**.

PERIMETER & AREA — *Rectilinear Shapes* — 68-69

16. The height of the shape is given by the two vertical sides on the left. $4+4 = \boxed{8}$.

The width of the rectilinear shape is 9. $9-5 = 4$, so $\boxed{4}+5 = 9$. The missing horizontal side length is 4.

17. We add all side lengths to find the perimeter: $9+4+5+4+4+8 = \mathbf{34}$.

18. The three horizontal sides on the bottom add up to $4+9+5 = 18$, so the length of the top of the shape must be 18.

To find the missing length of the short vertical side, we add the line below to create a 4 by 9 rectangle. The missing side length is the same as the opposite side of the rectangle: $\boxed{4}$.

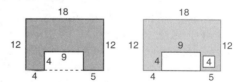

Now we can add all of the sides to get the perimeter: $(12+4+4)+(12+18)+(9+4+5) = 20+30+18 = \mathbf{68}$.

19. The two horizontal sides on top add up to $6+2 = 8$, so the horizontal sides on the bottom must also add up to 8. The two sides on the left add up to $6+2 = 8$, so the three sides on the right must also add up to 8. The perimeter of this shape is the same as an 8 by 8 square:

Perimeter $= 8+8+8+8 = \mathbf{32}$.

20. The width of the rectilinear shape is 14.
$3+7+\boxed{4}=14$, so the missing length on the horizontal side is 4. The height of the rectilinear shape is 9.
$2+3+\boxed{4}=9$, so the missing length on the vertical side is also 4.

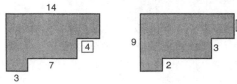

We can add the lengths of all 8 sides to get the perimeter: $2+3+4+9+3+7+4+14=\textbf{46}$.

— *or* —

We can find the perimeter without finding the missing side lengths. The short sides on the right side of the figure must add up to 9, and the short sides on the bottom of the figure must add up to 14, so the perimeter of the shape is the same as the perimeter of a 9 by 14 rectangle:

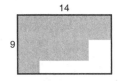

$9+14+9+14=(9+14)+(9+14)=23+23=\textbf{46}$.

21. $5+5+3=13$ and $6+4+3=13$, so this figure has the same perimeter as a 13 by 13 square:

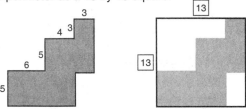

Perimeter $=(13+13)+(13+13)=26+26=\textbf{52}$.

22. We can find the height of the shape by adding the two vertical sides on the left: $9+4=13$. There is a missing horizontal length on top and a missing horizontal length on the bottom, so we cannot find the width of the figure. **Without knowing the width of the shape, it is not possible to find the perimeter of the shape**.

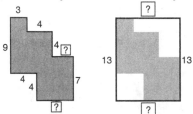

PERIMETER & AREA
Review 70-71

23. $(8+5)+(8+5)=13+13=\textbf{26}$.

24. $4+4+4+4+4+4=\textbf{24}$.

25. $(4+6)+7+(8+12)=10+7+20=\textbf{37}$.

26. $(4+6)+(3+7)+(8+2)+(4+6)+8$
$=10+10+10+10+8=\textbf{48}$.

27. $8+8+5+7+7+8+6+7=\textbf{56}$.

28. The length of the right side of the shape can be found by adding the lengths of the three short vertical sides on the left: $3+4+3=10$.

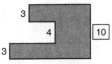

To find the other missing side length, split the rectilinear shape into three rectangles as shown.

Opposite sides of a rectangle have equal length:

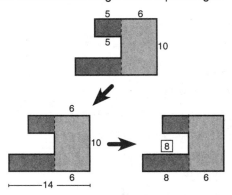

Now, we have enough information to find the perimeter:

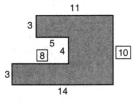

$11+10+14+3+8+4+5+3=\textbf{58}$.
This not the only way to split the shape into rectangles to find the missing side lengths. See if you can find another one.

29. Perimeter of Alex's "A":
$6+13+3+7+4+7+3+13$
$=(13+7)+(13+7)+(6+4)+(3+3)$
$=20+20+10+6$
$=56$.

Perimeter of Grogg's "G":
$12+10+4+8+8+6+5+5+8+14$
$=(12+8)+10+(4+8+8)+(6+14)+(5+5)$
$=20+10+20+20+10$
$=80$.

Perimeter of Winnie's "W":
$7+13+4+7+6+6+7+4+13+7$
$=(7+13)+(7+13)+(4+6)+(4+6)+7+7$
$=20+20+10+10+7+7$
$=74$.

Grogg's "G" has the greatest perimeter.

30. Lizzie's "L" has the same perimeter as an 18 by 17 rectangle.

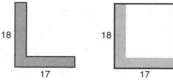

Perimeter = $(17+18)+(17+18) = 35+35 = 70$.

The perimeter of Lizzie's "L" is greater than the perimeters of Alex's "A", but less than the perimeter of Grogg's "G" and Winnie's "W".

PERIMETER & AREA
Missing Side Lengths　　72-73

31.
$9+16+15+\boxed{} = 51.$
$40+\boxed{} = 51.$
$51-40 = 11$, so $40+\boxed{11} = 51.$

32.
$13+10+8+12+\boxed{} = 50.$
$43+\boxed{} = 50.$
$50-43 = 7$, so $43+\boxed{7} = 50.$

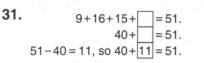

33.
$15+16+7+\boxed{} = 42.$
$38+\boxed{} = 42.$
$42-38 = 4$, so $38+\boxed{4} = 42.$

34.
$8+6+12+16+\boxed{} = 49.$
$42+\boxed{} = 49.$
$49-42 = 7$, so $42+\boxed{7} = 49.$

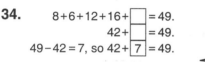

35.
$7+5+10+10+15+\boxed{} = 55.$
$47+\boxed{} = 55.$
$55-47 = 8$, so $47+\boxed{8} = 55.$

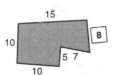

36.
$14+6+8+12+6+4+\boxed{} = 60.$
$50+\boxed{} = 60.$
$60-50 = 10$, so $50+\boxed{10} = 60.$

37. The two side lengths that we know add up to $20+20 = 40$. The perimeter is 50, so the sum of the two missing side lengths is $50-40 = 10$. Because the shape is a rectangle, the left and right side lengths both equal the height of the rectangle. We look for a number that can be added to itself to give us 10. Since $5+5 = 10$, the height of the rectangle is **5**.

PERIMETER & AREA
Word Problems　　74-77

38. $1+1+3+4+4+5 = \mathbf{18}.$

39. Four of the sticks are 3 inches long. This gives us $3+3+3+3 = 12$ inches. The perimeter of the pentagon is 16 inches, so length of the fifth stick is $16-12 = \mathbf{4\ inches}$.

40. There are many possibilities! Here are two examples:

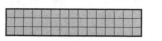

41. The two side lengths that we know add up to $7+7 = 14$. The perimeter is 20, so the sum of the two missing side lengths is $20-14 = 6$. Because the shape is a rectangle, the left and right side lengths both equal the height of the rectangle. We look for a number that can be added to itself to give us 6. Since $3+3 = 6$, the height of the rectangle is 3.

42. Below are the **7** rectangles that have whole-number side lengths and a perimeter of 16:

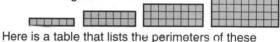

43. We can look at the perimeter of some rectangles with whole-number side lengths and whose widths are 5 more than their height.

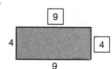

Here is a table that lists the perimeters of these rectangles:

Height	1	2	3	4	...
Width	6	7	8	9	...
Perimeter	14	18	22	26	...

The rectangle with height 2 and width 7 has a perimeter between 15 and 20. Any rectangle with a height greater than 3 and width greater than 8 has perimeter greater than 22, so the 2 by 7 rectangle is the only possible solution:

44.

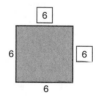

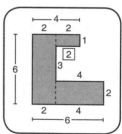

Perimeter = $(9+4)+(9+4) = 13+13 = 26$.　　Perimeter = $6+6+6+6 = 24$.

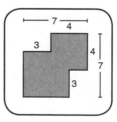

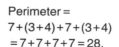

Perimeter = $7+(3+4)+7+(3+4)$ $= 7+7+7+7 = 28$.

Perimeter = $(6+4)+(6+4)+1+2+3+2$ $= 10+10+1+2+3+2 = 28$.

45. When we add one inch to the height of a rectangle, the lengths of its two vertical sides *each* increase by one inch.

The horizontal lengths do not change, so the perimeter of the rectangle increases by $1+1=2$ inches. Lizzie's rectangle has a perimeter that is 2 inches greater than the perimeter of Alex's rectangle: $18+2=$ **20 inches**.

46. When we make a rectangle 3 inches taller, the length of each vertical side increases by 3 inches. So, the perimeter increases by $3+3=6$ inches.

When we make a rectangle 1 inch wider, the length of each horizontal side increases by one inch, and the perimeter increases by $1+1=2$ inches.

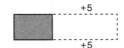

Therefore, Grogg's rectangle has a perimeter that is $6+2=8$ inches greater than the perimeter of Winnie's rectangle: $26+8=$ **34 inches**.

47. When you increase the width of a rectangle by 5 inches, you increase its perimeter by $5+5=10$ inches.

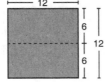

Since the perimeter of the new rectangle is 10 inches greater than the perimeter of the original rectangle, the perimeter of the original rectangle is 10 inches less than the perimeter of the new rectangle. The new rectangle has a perimeter of 22 inches, so the original rectangle has a perimeter of $22-10=$ **12 inches**.

48. The width of each rectangle is the same as the width of the square: 12. Because the rectangles are identical, the height of each rectangle is half the height of the square. Half of 12 is 6, so the height of each rectangle is 6.

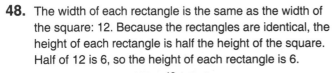

The perimeter of one 12 by 6 rectangle is $(12+6)+(12+6)=18+18=$ **36**.

49. The original square has a perimeter of 40, so it has sides of length 10, because $10+10+10+10=40$. The side length of each smaller square is half the side length of the original square. Half of 10 is 5.

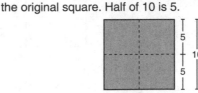

The perimeter of a square with sides of length 5 is $5+5+5+5=$ **20**.

50. The height of each identical rectangle is equal to the side length of the square. The width of each rectangle is half the side length of the square. Therefore, the width of each rectangle is half its height. We look for a rectangle with a perimeter of 24 whose width is half its height:

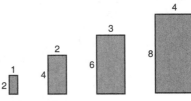

The 4 by 8 rectangle has a perimeter of 24 and a width that is half its height. The sides of the square are the same as the height of the rectangle, so the square has sides of length 8:

The square's perimeter is $8+8+8+8=$ **32**.

51. There are 12 sides of length 1. The perimeter is **12**.

52. **When we attach two heptagons, the two sides that meet are no longer part of the new shape's perimeter,** which is why the perimeter of the new figure is *two less* than the added perimeters of two separate heptagons.

53. There are 17 sides with length 1. The perimeter is **17**.

54. We found above that the perimeter of the 3-heptagon shape is 17. A 4-heptagon shape like the one drawn below has 22 sides of length 1 for a perimeter of 22:

$22-17=5$. So, the perimeter of the 4-heptagon shape is greater than the perimeter of the 3-heptagon shape by **5**.

— *or* —

Each time we attach a new heptagon to the shape, six sides of the new heptagon become part of new shape's perimeter (all but the one shared with the original shape). The new heptagon also covers one side of the original shape, removing it from the perimeter of the new shape. Therefore, the perimeter increases by 6−1 = **5**.

55. We explained above that each additional heptagon adds 5 to the perimeter. We know that the perimeter of a 4-heptagon shape is 22, so the 5-heptagon shape has perimeter 22+5 = 27. The 6-heptagon shape has perimeter 27+5 = 32. The 7-heptagon shape has perimeter 32+5 = 37, and the 8-heptagon shape has perimeter 37+5 = **42**.

— *or* —

We can attach two 4-heptagon shapes. Each 4-heptagon shape has a perimeter of 22. The two sides where they meet are not part of the new shape's perimeter, so the total perimeter of the 8-heptagon shape is 22+22−2 = **42**.

56. Each triangle has 3 sides, and it takes 6 of those sides to make the perimeter of the quadrilateral.

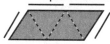

If we double the number of sides, then we double the perimeter. Since the perimeter of each triangle is 4, the perimeter of the quadrilateral is 4+4 = **8**.

57. Each hexagon has 6 sides, and it takes 12 of those sides to make the perimeter of the new shape.
If we double the number of sides, then we double the perimeter. Since the perimeter of each hexagon is 8, the perimeter of the new shape is 8+8 = **16**.

58. Each hexagon has 6 sides, and it takes 18 of those sides to make the perimeter of the new shape. 6+6+6 = 18, so this is the same as the number of sides in three hexagons. Since the perimeter of each hexagon is 5, the perimeter of the new shape is 5+5+5 = **15**.

59. Each square has 4 sides, and it takes 12 of those sides to make the perimeter of the new shape. 4+4+4 = 12, so this is the same as the number of sides in three squares. Since the perimeter of each square is 7, the perimeter of the new shape is 7+7+7 = **21**.

60. Each pentagon has 5 sides, and it takes 20 of those sides to make the perimeter of the new shape. 5+5+5+5 = 20, so this is the same as the number of sides in four pentagons. Since the perimeter of each hexagon is 12, the perimeter of the new shape is 12+12+12+12 = **48**.

61. The greatest possible distance from Grogg's house to the park occurs if Alex's house is directly between Grogg's house and the park:

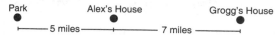

The greatest possible distance between Grogg's house and the park is 5+7 = **12 miles**.

62. The shortest possible distance from Grogg's house to the park occurs if the park is directly between Grogg's and Alex's houses:

The shortest possible distance between Grogg's house and the park is 7−5 = **2 miles**.

63. The top of the pole will be closest to the school entrance if the pole falls directly toward the door:

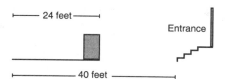

The closest that the top of the pole could land to the school entrance is 40−24 = **16 feet**.

64. The top of the pole will be farthest from the school entrance if the pole falls directly away from the door:

The farthest that the top of the pole could land from the school entrance is 24+40 = **64 feet**.

65. In Problems 63 and 64, we found that the top of the pole cannot be closer than 16 feet or farther than 64 feet from the school entrance. This eliminates two choices, and leaves us with two possible distances:

10 feet ⟨30 feet⟩ ⟨50 feet⟩ 70 feet

66. The sum of the two shortest sides of a triangle must be greater than the length of the longest side. If 7 is the longest side of the triangle, then the third side must be longer than 7−4 = 3 feet. If the third side of the flag is the longest, it must be shorter than 4+7 = 11 feet.

The third side of Kraken's flag must be longer than **3** feet, but shorter than **11** feet.

67. In the previous problem, we found that the third side must be longer than 3 feet and shorter than 11 feet. This eliminates two choices, and leaves us with 4 possible lengths.

2 feet ⟨4 feet⟩ ⟨6 feet⟩ ⟨8 feet⟩ ⟨10 feet⟩ 12 feet

68. We know that the length of the third side must be longer than 3 feet and shorter than 11 feet, so the perimeter of the flag must be *greater than* $4+7+3 = 14$ feet and *less than* $4+7+11 = 22$ feet. This eliminates 4 choices, and leaves us with 2 possible perimeters:

13 feet 16 feet 19 feet 22 feet 24 feet 25 feet

69. We check each group of poles:

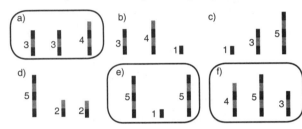

a) $3+3 = 6$ is more than 4.   b) $1+3 = 4$ is not more than 4.

c) $1+3 = 4$ is not more than 5.   d) $2+2 = 4$ is not more than 5.

e) $1+5 = 6$ is more than 5.   f) $3+4 = 7$ is more than 5.

We can only make a triangle from groups a, e, and f:

70. Because the triangle is isosceles, two of its sides are the same length. So, the length of the third side may only be 3 or 7. Since $3+3 = 6$ is *not* more than 7, the length of the third side cannot be 3.

$3+7 = 10$ is more than 7, so the length of the third side *could* be 7.

This is the only possible triangle, and the perimeter of this triangle is $7+7+3 = \textbf{17}$.

PERIMETER & AREA
Rectangles
83

71. $7+7 = \textbf{14 squares}$.

72. $4+4+4+4 = \textbf{16 squares}$.

73. $5+5+5+5 = \textbf{20 squares}$.

74. $8+8+8 = \textbf{24 squares}$.

75.

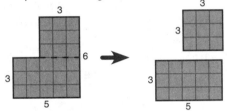

Area $= 6+6+6+6+6 = \textbf{30 squares}$.

76.

Area $= 7+7+7 = \textbf{21 squares}$.

PERIMETER & AREA
Rectilinear Shapes
84-85

These are not the only ways to split the shapes into rectangles!

77. Split the shape into rectangles:

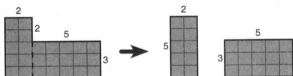

The 3 by 3 square has an area of $3+3+3 = 9$ squares.
The 3 by 5 rectangle has an area of $5+5+5 = 15$ squares.
The area of the original shape is $9+15 = \textbf{24 squares}$.

78. Split the shape into rectangles:

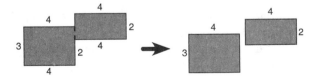

The 5 by 2 rectangle has an area of $5+5 = 10$ squares.
The 3 by 5 rectangle has an area of $5+5+5 = 15$ squares.
The area of the original shape is $10+15 = \textbf{25 squares}$.

79. Split the shape into rectangles:

The 3 by 4 rectangle has an area of $4+4+4 = 12$ squares.
The 2 by 4 rectangle has an area of $4+4 = 8$ squares.
The area of the original shape is $12+8 = \textbf{20 squares}$.

80. Split the shape into rectangles:

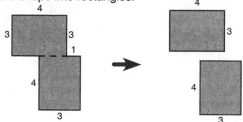

The area of the 3 by 4 rectangle is $4+4+4=12$ squares. The area of the 4 by 3 rectangle is $3+3+3+3=12$ squares. The area of the original shape is $12+12=\textbf{24 squares}$.

81. Notice that this shape's area is one square less than the area of a 5 by 5 square:

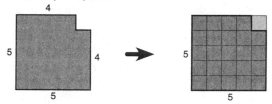

The area of the original shape is $(5+5+5+5+5)-1=25-1=\textbf{24 squares}$.

82. The area of this shape is 2 squares less than the area of a 6 by 6 square:

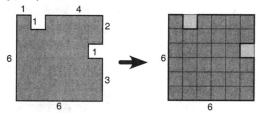

The area of the original shape is $(6+6+6+6+6+6)-2=36-2=\textbf{34 squares}$.

83. Split the shape into rectangles:

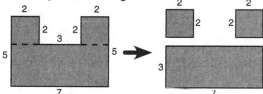

The area of the 3 by 7 rectangle is $7+7+7=21$ squares. The area of each 2 by 2 square is $2+2=4$ squares. The area of the original shape is $21+4+4=\textbf{29 squares}$.

— *or* —

We could find the area of a 5 by 7 rectangle and subtract the area of a 2 by 3 rectangle:

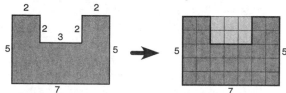

The area of a 5 by 7 rectangle is $7+7+7+7+7=35$ squares. The area of a 2 by 3 rectangle is $3+3=6$ squares. The area of the original shape is $35-6=\textbf{29 squares}$.

84. Split the shape into rectangles:

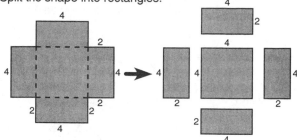

The area of each 2 by 4 and 4 by 2 rectangle is $4+4=8$ squares. The area of the 4 by 4 square is $4+4+4+4=16$ squares. The area of the original shape is $(8+8+8+8)+16=32+16=\textbf{48 squares}$.

— *or* —

The shape has the same area as an 8 by 8 square, minus four 2 by 2 squares:

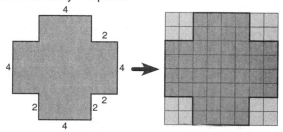

The area of the 8 by 8 square has an area of $8+8+8+8+8+8+8+8=64$ squares. Each 2 by 2 square has an area of $2+2=4$ squares. The total area of the original shape is $64-4-4-4-4=64-16=\textbf{48 squares}$.

85. We can split the shape as follows:

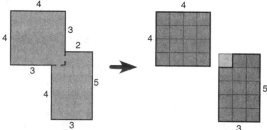

The 4 by 4 square has area $4+4+4+4=16$ squares. The area of the other shape is 1 less than the area of a 5 by 3 rectangle: $(5+5+5)-1=15-1=14$ squares. The area of the original shape is $16+14=\textbf{30 squares}$.

— *or* —

The shape has the same area as an 8 by 6 rectangle, minus a 4 by 3 rectangle and a 3 by 2 rectangle.

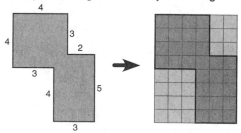

The area of an 8 by 6 rectangle is $8+8+8+8+8+8=48$ squares. The area of a 4 by 3 rectangle is $4+4+4=12$ squares. The area of a 3 by 2 rectangle is $3+3=6$ squares. The area of the original shape is $48-12-6=\textbf{30 squares}$.

86. We can split the shape as follows:

The area of the first shape left is one square less than the area of a 4 by 4 square: $(4+4+4+4)-1 = 16-1 = 15$ squares. The area of the 3 by 2 rectangle is $3+3 = 6$ squares. The area of the 5 by 3 rectangle is $5+5+5 = 15$ squares. The area of the original shape is $15+6+15 = $ **36 squares**.

87. A square with a perimeter of 20 has sides of length 5, because $5+5+5+5 = 20$. The area of a 5 by 5 square is $5+5+5+5+5 = $ **25 squares**.

88. A rectangle with perimeter of 18 and width 7 has height 2, because $7+2+7+2 = 18$. The area of a rectangle with height 2 and width 7 is $7+7 = $ **14 squares**.

89. There are two rectangles with whole-number side lengths and an area of 11: a rectangle with height 1 and width 11, or a rectangle with height 11 and width 1. The perimeter of a 1 by 11 rectangle is the same as the perimeter of an 11 by 1 rectangle: $(11+1)+(11+1) = 12+12 = $ **24**.

90. Below are the perimeters of the six rectangles.

1 by 12 and 12 by 1: $(1+12)+(1+12) = 13+13 = 26$,
2 by 6 and 6 by 2: $(2+6)+(2+6) = 8+8 = 16$, and
3 by 4 and 4 by 3: $(3+4)+(3+4) = 7+7 = 14$.

The perimeter of the 12 by 1 rectangle (and the 1 by 12 rectangle) is the largest: **26**.

91. Looking at the perimeters we found above, we see that the 3 by 4 rectangle (and the 4 by 3 rectangle) has the smallest perimeter: $3+4+3+4 = $ **14**.

92. Below are the five rectangles with whole-number side lengths and a perimeter of 12:

93. Of the rectangles above, the rectangle with the largest area is the 3 by 3 square, whose area is $3+3+3 = $ **9 squares**.

94. Of the rectangles above, the rectangles with the smallest area are the 1 by 5 rectangle and the 5 by 1 rectangle. The area of each of those rectangles is **5 squares**.

95. The perimeter of the shape is **20**.

96. The area of the shape is **15 squares**.

97. If we add the darkly shaded square as shown below, we eliminate 3 sides from the perimeter and add only 1 side. This decreases the perimeter of the shape by 2, from 20 to 18.

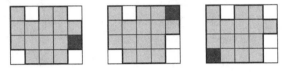

98. Each of the three darkly shaded squares below covers 2 existing sides and adds 2 new sides to the perimeter of the original shape, leaving the perimeter unchanged.

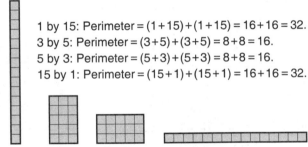

99. You may have traced one of four possible rectangles that has an area of 15:

1 by 15: Perimeter $= (1+15)+(1+15) = 16+16 = 32$.
3 by 5: Perimeter $= (3+5)+(3+5) = 8+8 = 16$.
5 by 3: Perimeter $= (5+3)+(5+3) = 8+8 = 16$.
15 by 1: Perimeter $= (15+1)+(15+1) = 16+16 = 32$.

If you drew the 1 by 15 rectangle or the 15 by 1 rectangle, the perimeter of your rectangle is **larger** than the perimeter of Winnie's shape.

If you drew the 3 by 5 rectangle or the 5 by 3 rectangle, the perimeter of your rectangle is **smaller** than the perimeter of Winnie's shape.

100. We want to find rectangles with area larger than 15 squares and perimeter smaller than 20. You may have drawn any of the following rectangles:

Height	3	4	4	5	6
Width	6	4	5	4	3
Perimeter	18	16	18	18	18
Area (in squares)	18	16	20	20	18

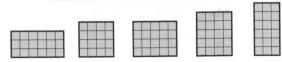

Challenge: The 4 by 5 and the 5 by 4 rectangles have an area of 20 squares, which is the largest area among the rectangles whose perimeter is smaller than Winnie's shape.

101. We want to find rectangles with perimeter greater than 20 and area smaller than 15 squares. You may have drawn any of the following rectangles:

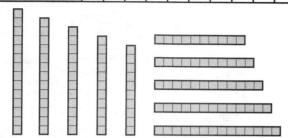

Height	1	1	1	1	1	10	11	12	13	14
Width	10	11	12	13	14	1	1	1	1	1
Perimeter	22	24	26	28	30	22	24	26	28	30
Area (in squares)	10	11	12	13	14	10	11	12	13	14

Challenge: The 14 by 1 and 1 by 14 rectangle have a perimeter of 30, which is the largest perimeter among the rectangles whose area is smaller than Winnie's shape.

102. **False**. For example, in Problem 98, we can increase the area of Winnie's shape without changing its perimeter. Also, two shapes that have the same area do not always have the same perimeter. In Problem 99, you drew a rectangle with the same area as Winnie's shape, but its perimeter was different.

103. **False**. The rectangles in Problem 100 have a larger area but smaller perimeter than Winnie's shape.

104. **False**. The rectangles in Problem 101 have a larger perimeter but smaller area than Winnie's shape.

105. Each smaller square has a perimeter of 12, so the small squares have side length 3 because $3+3+3+3=12$. Each side of the larger square is double the length of one side of a small square: $3+3=6$.

The area of a 6 by 6 square is $6+6+6+6+6+6=$ **36 squares**.

— *or* —

Each small square has an area of $3+3+3=9$ squares.

The large square is made up of 4 small squares, so we add 9 four times to find its area: $9+9+9+9=$ **36 squares**.

106. If the three rectangles are connected to form a square, the resulting square's area will be equal to the combined areas of all the rectangles: $3+10+12=25$ squares. A square with an area of 25 squares has side length 5, because $5+5+5+5+5=25$. The perimeter of the square is $5+5+5+5=$ **20**.

— *or* —

Draw and arrange the rectangles. Here is one way:

We could have also drawn the rectangles flipped or turned in different directions. In each drawing, we get a square with side length 5. The perimeter of the square is $5+5+5+5=$ **20**.

107. We first draw the shape described. The shape below is the only shape that fits the description given.

To find its area, we can see that this shape is made of five 2 by 2 squares, each with area $2+2=4$ squares:

The area of the shape is $4+4+4+4+4=$ **20 squares**.

108. The top rectangle has a perimeter of $(5+1)+(5+1)=6+6=12$. The bottom rectangle has a perimeter of $(5+2)+(5+2)=7+7=14$.

The total perimeter of the rectangles is $12+14=$ **26**.

— *or* —

This straight cut makes two rectangles. Each new rectangle has one side of length 5 created by the straight cut (the bolded lines). The total perimeter of the two new rectangles includes the perimeter of the original rectangle plus the lengths of the sides created by the cut. We can find the total perimeter by adding the perimeter of the original rectangle and twice the length of the cut. The perimeter of the original rectangle is 16, and the length of the cut is 5. The total perimeter of the two new rectangles is $16+(5+5)=16+10=$ **26**.

109. The polygon to the left has a perimeter of 14. The polygon to the right also has a perimeter of 14.

The total perimeter of the shapes is $14+14 = \mathbf{28}$.

— *or* —

The squiggle cut makes two new shapes. Each new shape has some sides created by the squiggle cut (the bolded lines). The total perimeter of the two new shapes includes the perimeter of the original rectangle, plus the lengths of the sides created by the cut.

We can find the total perimeter by adding the perimeter of the original rectangle and twice the length of the cut. The perimeter of the original rectangle is 16, and the length of the cut is 6. The total perimeter of the two new rectangles is $16+(6+6) = 16+12 = \mathbf{28}$.

110. Grogg could have split the rectangles with either a vertical straight cut or a horizontal straight cut. A horizontal straight cut will have length 5, so the total perimeter of the two new rectangles will be $16+(5+5) = 16+10 = 26$.

A vertical straight cut will have length 3, so the total perimeter of the two new rectangles will be $16+(3+3) = 16+6 = 22$.

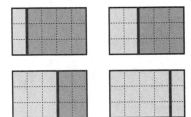

Any of the vertical cuts will give the smallest total perimeter: **22**.

111. A longer cut will give us polygons with a greater total perimeter, so we make the longest cut we can. The longest squiggle that splits the shape into two polygons has length 9. Below are some possible squiggle cuts of length 9:

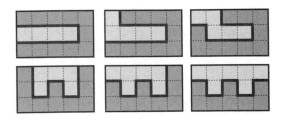

The greatest possible total perimeter the two shapes is $16+(9+9) = 16+18 = \mathbf{34}$.

112. The perimeter of the original rectilinear shape is 16.

If the straight cut shown to the right is made, the total perimeter of the two polygons is $16+(2+2) = 16+4 = 20$.

If any of the following three cuts are made, the total perimeter of the two polygons is $16+(3+3) = 16+6 = 22$.

If the straight cut shown to the right is made, the total perimeter of the two polygons is $16+(4+4) = 16+8 = 24$.

If the straight cut shown to the right is made, the total perimeter of the two polygons is $16+(5+5) = 16+10 = 26$.

Therefore, the four possible values for the total perimeter of the polygons split by one straight cut are **20**, **22**, **24**, and **26**.

113. There are four possible squiggle cuts that split the shape into two polygons with equal perimeter. Each of the squiggle cuts below produces two polygons with a perimeter of 12.

Each squiggle cut below produces two polygons with a perimeter of 14.

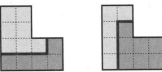

Notice that each of the two polygons has *half* of the boundary of the original shape.

114. There are many ways to split the shape into three polygons with the same perimeter. Two ways to split the shape into three polygons, each with perimeter 10, are shown below:

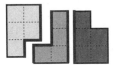

Challenge: Below are two possible ways to split the shape into four polygons, each with perimeter 8.

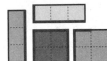

115. There are many ways to do this. Below are two possible ways to split the shape into three polygons with a perimeter of 10, each with a different area. In each, one shape has an area of 4 squares, another has an area of 5 squares, and the area of the third shape is 6 squares.

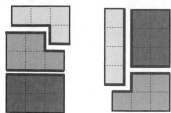

For additional books, printables, and more, visit
www.BeastAcademy.com